ESHERICK HOMSEY DODGE & DAVIS

EHDD BUILDING BEYOND THE BAY

ESHERICK HOMSEY DODGE & DAVIS

EHDD BUILDING BEYOND THE BAY

INTRODUCTORY ESSAYS

FEATURE PROJECTS

MONTEREY BAY AQUARIUM

UNIVERSITY OF CALIFORNIA

First published in the United States of America by Edizioni Press, Inc., 469 West 21st Street, New York, New York 10011, Mail@edizionipress.com
ISBN:1-931536-02-3 Library of Congress Catalogue Card Number: 2001092440 Printed in Italy
Design: Claudia Brandenburg; Assistant Editors: Sarah Palmer, Jamie Schwartz; Editorial Assistants: Kara Janeczko, Aaron Seward; Cover photo by Peter Aaron/ESTO; Endpaper photo by Lindsey Adelman

FROM REGIONALISM TO INTERNATIONAL

For many architects, the name Joseph Esherick is almost synonymous with the Hedgerow Houses at Sea Ranch, the modest but influential residential community designed with Charles Moore and Lawrence Halprin that gave form to the spirit of regionalism and humanism of the mid 1960s. But to look at Esherick's firm—now called Esherick Homsey Dodge & Davis and known by its more commercial-sounding acronym, EHDD—almost 40 years after Sea Ranch is to see a completely different kind of practice. To understand what shaped its history is to understand how it has evolved in scope and size.

EHDD spent its early years successfully marrying the budding Bay Area traditions of wood buildings established by predecessors such as Bernard Maybeck and Willis Polk with a more universal notion of modern space. In fact, the firm was in many ways the embodiment of early Bay Area modernism. In the late 1970s and 80s, the designers of comfortable California living became experts in the field of aquarium architecture, following their landmark work on the Monterey Bay Aquarium. Today, however, the firm is a multi-office operation with studios in San Francisco, Monterey, and Chicago; clients across the country and abroad; and a mix of client and building types. How does a firm evolve from small-scale region-alist, to large-scale specialist, to a successful multi-discipline firm?

It is quite likely because the same skills and attitudes that brought EHDD success in the early days have helped the firm achieve its present stature. Even though the Bay Area regionalism Joseph Esherick helped bring to life eventually became known more by its stylistic than philosophical overtones, it was not conceived as a formal style. Esherick, like other East Coast–trained architects who headed west in the first half of the 20th century, distilled architecture to what he considered the essence of California living: informal structures, usually built of local wood, that responded to basics of the site, the light, and the mild climate. These gentle buildings framed special views, preserved existing vegetation, and were inherently concerned with conserving energy through common-sense means. He made buildings seem part of their site, natural extensions of the California landscape. In short, following this regionalist attitude, Esherick made the most of the best parts of

a project and its site—an approach that translates to any number of commissions.

Many of EHDD's current projects draw on this same sensitivity to place. Projects such as the science library at the University of California, Santa Cruz, reveal similar thinking to the firm's earliest California buildings, what Esherick's contemporary and collaborator Charles Moore praised as "laying lightly on the land." At Santa Cruz, the architects moved hardly so much as a tree, opened up the library to the densely forested surroundings with huge expanses of glass, and threaded outdoor walkways among the trees. Sustainability takes center stage perhaps more than in any other EHDD project in the 1001 Emerson house, a live-in residential laboratory built with energy efficient strategies in mind. These two projects demonstrate that while EHDD has grown, it still takes to heart the principles that put its design on the map in the first place.

EHDD made a giant leap in size and geographic range from their early work—mostly houses and buildings for local institutions—after mastering a single building type: the aquarium. The break-through project was a marine laboratory at the University of California, Santa Cruz, which EHDD principal Marc L'Italien discusses in his introductory text to this volume. This laboratory planted the seed for EHDD's eventual commission for the Monterey Bay Aquarium, which truly elevated the firm to experts in this complex building type.

In the late 1960s and early 80s, landmark projects such as the New England Aquarium on Boston Harbor and the National Aquarium in Baltimore defined the contemporary aquarium and raised public interest in the building type. But the architects of these modern aquariums, in the service of meeting complex technical and functional requirements, created concrete icons out of scale and character with their urban neighbors. These buildings helped revitalize urban waterfront areas (in fact, Baltimore's aquarium did much to boost the entire city), but they weren't successfully integrated into the urban fabric.

EHDD, by comparison, proved that a functional, state-of-the-art aquarium could, indeed, fit seamlessly into its context, whether the picturesque waterfront of Monterey, California, or the venerable

PRACTICE RAUL A. BARRENECHE

neoclassical shell of Chicago's lakefront Shedd Aquarium. And further, their designs successfully integrate commercial aspects that are becoming an increasingly important financial requisite in museums and other large public institutions, including aquariums. Not only must the architects organize complex behind-the-scenes systems and design polished, functional front-of-house spaces, but they must also create visually enticing shops that bring in much-needed revenue. As in their early projects, EHDD's aquariums reveal an ability to address pragmatic issues while creating meaningful, sensitive buildings. These buildings prove that for them function does not take precedence over form, nor does style overwhelm substance.

Though they have achieved great success with this single building type, EHDD has not been mired in aquariums. Unlike other firms, they are at once synonymous with mastery of a certain kind of project, but also associated with a range of building types. Their work has not been limited by type or geography because the architects have been able to apply their problem-solving instincts—an integral part of the firm's history and a part of what Chuck Davis calls "the expanded solution" in Marc L'Italien's closing essay to this volume—to a range of projects and places, including schools, offices, and libraries, both close to San Francisco and far from home.

EHDD's architects are aware of precedent but unencumbered by the past. They have a strong sense of the traditions of their firm, but also of innovation and investigation—skills that have taken EHDD from its strong regional roots to a truly international practice. Though they have grown much beyond Sea Ranch, it still looms large in their psyche.

BEYOND THE BAY MARC L'ITALIEN

Esherick Homsey Dodge & Davis creates ordinary architecture. As Jaques Leslie wrote in *The New York Times*, the firm maintains a long tradition of designing understated, self-effacing buildings, claiming that the ideal building is one you don't see, one that blends into its environment. Their work, exquisitely proportioned and detailed, has an honesty of expression that belies the notion that the architect's primary role is as maker of form.[1] EHDD's buildings celebrate the movement and activities of the inhabitants and users. They also provide a neutral armature for the program requirements and provide views that change depending on season, time of day, and position within a room. The designs emphasize a connection to, and respect for, the place that preceded the building. Principal Peter Dodge explains, "[EHDD] strives for something that satisfies and provides a reasonable experience for the person who has to work or live in a building....People who have spent 20 years in a building that we've designed have told us that the building continues to evolve for them and to be a profound satisfaction."[2]

EHDD practices in the Bay Region Style, a term coined by Louis Mumford that represents an attitude toward building in Northern California, around the San Francisco Bay. Seminal projects are direct in their use of materials, minimal in their construction of physical enclosures, and intent on creating a sense of shelter. In this benign climate, the projects emphasize the union of the architecture and the landscape, built or otherwise, and take advantage of breathtaking views. This tradition was a response to the mythical (and often factual) ideas about California as a veritable Promised Land. In his essay, "William Wilson Wurster: The Feeling of Function," Marc Trieb asserts that the Bay Region tradition promotes architecture that is free from historical precedent and appropriate to the environment.[3] For EHDD's founder, Joseph Esherick, the Bay Region, as opposed to New England, had a style that focused on internal attitude, rather than external form.[4]

Wurster's strong influence is evident in the following 1961 quote by Joseph Esherick: "Beauty
is a consequential thing, a byproduct of solving problems correctly. It is as unreal as the goal. Preoccupation with aesthetics leads to arbitrary design, to buildings that take a certain form because the designer 'likes the way it looks.' No successful architecture can be formulated on a generalized system of aesthetics; it must be based on a way of life. We must decide what is alive and vital in our culture and approach each problem with this in mind. By approaching things subjectively and in a materialistic way we will never learn what things are. We need to know what things are, and what they are for. We need to discover realities and meanings."[5]

Although EHDD has now expanded its work and offices beyond the Golden State, these principles remain high priorities. Investigations into regions with varying climates and terrains, as well as the client needs at hand, continue to inform design on all of the projects; aesthetics are the byproduct of this search. In 1945, Bay Area architect William Wurster wrote, "Architecture...should not be solely the self-expression of the architect. It is not an easel painting. It is a part of the life of the client and all those who look at it. A true test of the architect is whether he is serving the best interests of the client, and not the impossible whims of his own."[6]

EHDD pursues purely stylistic concerns only as far as they further the satisfaction of the client, the program, and the exigencies of the site; the firm is never concerned with the stylistic expression of the architect as form-maker and trendsetter. Endorsing EHDD for AIA's Firm of the Year, Robert Venturi once stated, "...[I]t is symbolically important... to recognize firms like EHDD that have been so instrumental in providing American architecture with great style and consistency, while all about them the architectural world gets lost, and starts and fads rise and fall."[7]

THE FOUNDING PRINCIPAL

Joseph Esherick, EHDD's founding principal, was raised and educated in Philadelphia. He traveled west in 1938, as had the first exponents of the Bay Area tradition around the turn of the century: Ernest Coxhead, Bernard Maybeck, and Willis Polk, who all came from environments very different than that of the Bay Area. Although Esherick studied under Paul Cret in the Beaux-Arts system at the University of Pennsylvania, he got hands-on training with his uncle, Wharton Esherick, a local wood sculptor, craftsman, and furniture maker, who approached design problems with the initial question: "How would a farmer do it?" In his 1994 *Texas Architect* article, "Life Work: The Architecture of Joseph Esherick," Frank D. Welch claimed that Wharton's attitude instilled in his nephew the habit of disregarding extraneous issues that can muddle the clarity of a design. The search for the simplest relationship between form and function would be important to Joseph Esherick throughout his life. [8]

Upon his arrival in San Francisco, Esherick approached William Wurster for a job, but was instead referred to Gardner Dailey, who, along with Wurster, was one of the leading Bay Area architects of the time. The East Coast establishment knew both architects for producing a warmer, more regional version of modernism, which was referred to, somewhat pejoratively, as the "woodsy Bay Region tradition" or the "International Cottage Style." While Wurster looked to the vernacular architecture of 19th-century California for inspiration in creating his lean, stripped-down forms, Dailey looked to the early architects of the Bay Region tradition. David Gebhard's essay, "William Wurster and His California Contemporaries: The Idea of Regionalism and Soft Modernism," explains that Dailey tended towards historicism and adventurous forms as they suited his projects. Esherick's debt to Dailey was evident in the vertical lines and the expression of roof forms in his designs, but his tendency towards planar forms and straightforward detailing were more akin to Wurster's design sensibilities. [9]

Joseph Esherick set up his own practice in 1946 and soon became known as one of the chief proponents of the post-war Bay Region tradition. The consistent work of George Homsey, Peter Dodge, and, the most recent recruit, Chuck Davis, on seminal projects was acknowledged by Esherick in 1963. He promoted the three men and changed the firm's name from "Joseph Esherick, Architect" to "Joseph Esherick and Associates." In 1972, Esherick's three associates became principals and the firm's name was changed to "Esherick Homsey Dodge & Davis."

The firm successfully expanded in scope, taking on larger commercial and institutional projects, and received a significant amount of recognition in the U.S., Europe, and Japan. In 1980, EHDD received the AIA California Council Firm Award; in 1986, the national AIA Firm of the Year Award. In 1989, Joseph Esherick was awarded the AIA Gold Medal.

The early projects gave Esherick the opportunity to consider his process and develop a method of working with clients whereby he could respond to their various concerns by sketching explanations on the spot, drawing the clients into the creative process. This is a working method rarely employed by architects today, but still used by EHDD.

PROJECTS

EARLY RESIDENTIAL COMMISSIONS

EHDD's earliest commissions were sited in the Sierras, on the shores of Lake Tahoe. The first project, the Metcalf House, is a wood frame dwelling, a simple, preconceived form into which the entire program is packed. The house displays the quintessential elements of the Bay Area tradition of architecture, namely the use of natural rustic elements. At the request of Mrs. Metcalf, extreme care was taken not to affect the fragile alpine vegetation on the property during construction. This was a concept foreign to builders of that period, but a lesson that would stay with Esherick as he and

his collaborators continued to build in the picturesque, yet fragile, California landscape.[10]

According to Suzanne Reiss, author of *Joseph Esherick: An Oral History: An Architectural Practice in the San Francisco Bay Area 1938-1996*, the parti for the Metcalf House materialized on the back of an envelope, as Esherick rode on a Greyhound bus. It was one of Esherick's only projects to even have a parti, and one of the few that was not developed by one of his future partners, under his direction.[11]

Soon, Esherick began experimenting with daylight, balancing the bright warm south light with cool northern light to minimize glare and maximize views to the outdoors. Without altering the mass, Esherick could indicate various interior functions using fenestration on the outside. In the Bradley House, corridors are avoided by the camp-like plan and all rooms have exterior access and a narrow width. This provides daylight exposure from two directions, while minimizing strong glare from the nearby lake. In houses built later, this balancing act was fine-tuned: the color and texture of wall surfaces were used to change the ambiance of interior spaces daily and seasonally.

During the postwar period, budgets were often modest and specific design elements were sometimes envisioned with more than one function in mind. In the Walker House, a wood slat panel beneath the second story summer deck folds down during the winter and becomes a great shutter that protects the view windows from the winds and deep snow of the Sierra winters. Unlike that of the simpler Metcalf House, the bracket structure supporting the roof here is expressed and sculpted.

The Goldman House was Esherick's first major urban residential project. Its simple form is reminiscent of the modest postwar houses of William Wurster. The house is spatially arranged to take advantage of views out to the bay. The design responds to the changing microclimate of the Pacific Heights district of San Francisco by providing a sheltered outdoor room on the building's leeward side and a rather forward-thinking radiant heat ceiling.

1 Metcalf House, Lake Tahoe, CA, 1948
   Photographer: Roy Flamm
2 Bradley House, Lake Tahoe, CA, 1948
   Photographer: Ernest Braun
3 Bradley House, Lake Tahoe, CA, 1948
   Photographer: Ernest Braun
4 Walker House, Lake Tahoe, CA, 1948
   Photographer unknown
5 Goldman House, San Francisco, CA, 1951
   Photographer: Morely Baer
6 McIntyre House, Hillsborough, CA, 1960
   Photographer: Ezra Stoller

In the February 1998 issue of *architecture + urbanism*, Ken Tadashi Oshima explained that Esherick had been moved by the low, mysterious light quality in Akira Kurosawa's film, *Rashomon*. He was able to achieve this effect in the Goldman House by maintaining a low light level from windows to the north and counteracting it with daylight from the south to eliminate glare.[12]

In his designs for the Goldman House, Esherick addresses the balance of light with a rooftop bubble skylight, the first of this type used in San Francisco. In the living room there is a gentle balance between northern and southern light, which minimizes the difference between the light levels inside and outside; this was a practical consideration, inspired by Gardner Dailey.

The Goldman House was perhaps the clearest example of packing the box. This was a term used by the firm to describe the challenge of composing a multitude of spaces into a simple, tight two-story volume; it is not unlike the challenges presented in fitting different types and sizes of rooms into the fixed volume of a ship. This packing approach was common to many of EHDD's houses through the mid 1950s, and would often culminate in the vertical extrusion of key spaces in the houses with no visible impact on the general building mass.

During the late 1950s, budgets increased for residential work. It was during this period that the hand of Esherick's collaborators became more evident. The designs also became more internally oriented, leaving the exterior a more complex and overt expression of the internal program. The earliest manifestation of this idea is seen in the McIntyre House. George Homsey assisted Esherick in the complex assembly of smaller modules that delineated accommodations for a growing family on the gently sloping site. The main feature of the house is a central atrium covered by a technical assembly of 20 plastic skylights set into a precast concrete roof frame, which doubles as a rainwater diversion system. This system was developed with the aid of structural engineer William Gilbert, of Gilbert Forsberg Diekman and Schmidt, and Western Art Stone, a statuary company hand-picked for the project. In a radical departure from earlier wood frame construction, the architects used an industrial concrete tilt-up system for the walls to speed erection time and aid in the individual expression of the various pavilions.

The origin of the formal break that occurred in the McIntyre House is not entirely clear. It has been speculated that Esherick modified an earlier design for the house after a trip to Philadelphia, where he visited Louis Kahn, a close friend of his uncle Wharton Esherick. At the time of Esherick's visit, Kahn's Richards Medical Laboratories project was in design. Richards was the first large-scale project in which Kahn more clearly differentiated the floor plan into servant and served spaces; a similar spatial breakdown is evident in the McIntyre plan. Because Kahn was also experimenting with precast concrete structural systems at that time, the correlation seems probable.

The next project to incorporate the concrete frame was the Bermak House, designed for an Oakland psychiatrist, Gordon Bermak, on a precipitous site in the Oakland Hills, which offered panoramic views of San Francisco and the bay. Bermak desired a house that would jut out into the landscape, perpendicular to the contours. Esherick called again on structural engineer William Gilbert to develop a concrete support structure that would solve the technical problems, without requiring the forest of columns typical of a

7

wood pier system. The resulting design gives a vertical appearance, due to the tall, slender concrete piers that support a concrete super-structure with wood frame infill. This project was concurrent with the firm's design work on Wurster Hall, future home of the College of Environmental Design at the University of California, Berkeley, the largest project undertaken by the firm up until this time, and one built entirely of concrete.

Photographer Roy Flamm noted that the completed Bermak House appeared to have been set down in its resting place by helicopter. [13]

In the early 1960s, Esherick designed two wood frame houses that broke from cladding approaches common in his residential work of the previous decade. The Cary House and the McLeod House, designed with Peter Dodge, do away with stucco, board and battens, and vertical wood siding. Here, smooth uninterrupted expanses of wood shingles appear to be stretched taut around the building mass; window apertures with minimal detailing appear to accommodate interior spaces, resisting any formal ordering system at the exterior.

Reiss asserts that Esherick was influenced by the paintings of Clifford Still and intrigued by the notion that a single window could manipulate an entire wall plane; this maneuver could radically change a space compositionally and spatially. He was also driven to examine the scale of the window, the window's capacity to admit light, and the ways a window might become a framed view to the outdoor scenery, which changed depending on one's vantage point within the room. [14]

The Cary House in Mill Valley has dramatic views of Mount Tamalpais. The site, the views, and the various interior functions drive the organization of the house. Its form is accented by the extensive use of exterior wood trellises, positioned to mitigate the harsh sunlight. In this project, skylights and windows were carefully positioned, in relation to interior wall partitions, in order to investigate the plastic qualities of the wall planes.

8   9

The McLeod House on Belvedere Island, overlooking Tiburon and the bay, is a more overt and developed example of shifting floor planes and ceiling heights, and the orientation of rooms and windows in response to the site. Here the roof is constructed of side-by-side 2x4s on edge, which are exposed as the finished ceiling surface. The extreme vertical proportions of the interior respond to the dramatic vista. The tall, elegant window proportions and the slender wall space between window units reach a clear level of refinement and expression that would not be repeated in any other project. Commenting on the dynamic spatial qualities of the house, Charles Moore wrote, "There is the sense that the architect plunged down

10 11

the steep hill past the oak to the marine view, gobbled it all up, and brought forth the house in chunks of light and outlook—the way the action painter flings his wet paint onto his canvas, then responds directly to it in whatever way the ensuing seconds seem to demand."[15]

THE SEA RANCH

During this same period, Lawrence Halprin chose Joseph Esherick and Associates and Charles Moore's firm, MLTW (Moore Lyndon Turnbull Whitaker), to design the first buildings at the Sea Ranch. The initial planning of this second-home resort community, sited on a former sheep ranch on the Mendocino coast, north of San Francisco, had been developed by Halprin for Oceanic Properties. MLTW was assigned the condominium project and Joseph Esherick, Architect, designed the general store and the Hedgerow Houses— six oceanfront demonstration houses built along a cypress hedgerow, overlooking an open meadow. These houses were the physical embodiment of the planning principles developed by Lawrence Halprin; they also expressed the straightforward architecture and sensitivity to the landscape promoted by Esherick and later discussed at length in the book by Charles Moore, Gerald Allen, and Donlyn Lyndon, *The Place of Houses*.

Each of the six wood frame houses in the cluster supports a sloping single shed roof, the pitch of which was calculated to channel the coastal winds up and over useable outdoor spaces situated on the south side of all the units. On two of the houses, sod was placed over a five-ply coal tar built-up roof to add mass and stabilize the structure so that it could withstand the wind. The rooftop grass camouflages the structures when they are viewed from across the meadow. The houses are set low to the ground, with the top of land berms at windowsill height, a gesture that further merges the houses with the native terrain. According to Donald Canty, the MLTW condominium was more assertive and fortress-like (in Moore's own words, "the architecture is in limited partnership with the land"), whereas the cluster houses seem to fuse with the landscape, particularly when seen in profile against the windblown cypress trees of the nearby hedgerow.[16]

The Sea Ranch general store was designed using the simple barn vernacular of the region. The program called for a small store to sell a variety of sundries and local implements, tailored to the specific needs of the Sea Ranch residents. It is now the Sea Ranch Development Office and the General Store, a structure that lacks the power and simplicity of the original Esherick building because it has been subsumed by a series of lesser additions and alterations.

12 13

EARLY UNIVERSITY WORK

While Joseph Esherick and Associates continued to practice residential architecture, its commissions began to shift in the 1960s from primarily residential to larger scale public and private buildings.

14

Wurster Hall, the College of Environmental Design at the University of California, Berkeley, was the first of these larger projects. College Dean William Wurster assembled a consortium of four architectural offices to collaborate on the project, including Hardison and Komatsu, De Mars & Reay, Donald Olsen, and Joseph Esherick and Associates. The final product, the first large-scale precast-clad concrete building in the Western United States, was ground-breaking in its technology, yet straightforward in its rational disposition of studios and manipulation of daylight.[17]

The sunshades in Wurster Hall, at the University of California, are similar in their articulation to those used in Le Corbusier's seminal projects at the Unite D'Habitation in Marseilles and at the Secretariat in Chandigarh, both built in the 1950s.

Because of its strong concrete form, it became somewhat of a landmark. In the 1960s, students adorned the southern façade of the tower with large snack food cutouts, rendering it the world's largest vending machine. Esherick was thrilled with the irreverent nature of these interpretations.

The firm's second major academic project came by way of Jack Wagstaff, the campus architect at the University of California, Santa Cruz, and a long time employee of Wurster Bernardi & Emmons. UC Santa Cruz was a rural campus set in a redwood forest and oceanfront meadow just north of the town. The campus was planned by John Carl Warnecke and Associates and Anshen + Allen; landscape architect Thomas Church was a consultant. The campus plan realized chancellor McHenry's dream of modeling UC Santa Cruz on Oxford and Cambridge Universities, where all the social and academic functions are integrated into several unique college units. Adlai E. Stevenson College, designed by Joseph Esherick and Associates, was the first college completed.

Stevenson College was designed in an informal residential scale so as not to overpower the natural environment or other buildings on campus. The slightly skewed siting not only enhances the views, but also creates a more sensitive relationship to the site. Student and faculty interaction was a primary concern, so the distinction of program between the various buildings is intentionally blurred. The shed-like academic buildings, concrete frame structures with wood infill, recall the firm's earlier residential work. The buildings are sheathed in stucco and feature clay tile

15

roofs. The three-story residential halls are traditional western wood frame construction.

The firm's next major campus project was the McPhee Union at California Polytechnic University, San Luis Obispo. The new building needed to provide a center of activity for the campus on a site that sits at the confluence of preexisting pedestrian circulation routes. The design provides for the uninterrupted movement of

14 Wurster Hall, College of Environmental
Design, University of California,
Berkeley, 1965
Photographer: Rondal Partridge

15 Adlai E. Stevenson College,
University of California, Santa Cruz, 1966
Photographer: Rondal Partridge

16 McPhee Union, California Polytechnic
Institute, San Luis Obispo, 1970
Photographer: Wayne Thom

17 The Cannery, San Francisco, CA, 1966
Photographer: Ernest Braun

16

people through the site and offers multiple points of entry. The new outdoor circulation space doubles as a street and a public assembly space, complete with amphitheater; McPhee is an Acropolis of sorts, defined as much by the outdoor precinct as by the buildings that embrace it.

The McPhee Union is a concrete frame building with masonry infill that responds to the change in elevation across the site with multiple level shifts. Long spans with Vierendeel trusses were incorporated into the design to accommodate a variety of indoor uses and provide for future flexibility. Here the daylight is controlled with large overhangs; this was a further iteration of the concrete sun-shades at Wurster Hall and the earlier wood trellises of the Cary and Bermak residences. Strong color was used extensively on the exterior and interior to enliven the public spaces and orient visitors.

COMMERCIAL WORK

Esherick's first foray into commercial work was the Cannery on San Francisco's Fisherman's Wharf. This project, designed with Peter Dodge, was one of the first completed adaptive reuse projects of its type on the West Coast. Ghirardelli Square, a project in the same vicinity, by Wurster Bernardi & Emmons, had been completed six months previously. Other similar warehouses in the area had fallen victim to the wrecking ball before Leonard Martin, a former residential client of Esherick's, approached him with an idea for an urban market-

place. The Cannery building had been a Del Monte canning factory and was being used as a parking garage when design work began.

In 1976, Charles Moore wrote an eloquent text praising Esherick for producing the Cannery, whose architecture is dedicated to the inhabitant, not to the maker of form and spatial climaxes. Seventeenth-century Japanese tea masters were able to understand the inherent beauty and value in objects as common as a teapot; Moore applauded Esherick for ritualizing the mundane in this project, calling him "a tea master who possesses the key to the super-aristocratic ritual of understatement..."[18]

The completed building is accessible from many points. A labyrinthine assemblage of outdoor and indoor spaces allows a continuous flow of pedestrian traffic to permeate the complex.

17

The outside spaces, intended for public interaction and assembly, are sheltered from the winds off of San Francisco Bay and are given a status equivalent to that of the leased spaces within the design. Formal axial progressions were avoided to encourage random access; the design accentuates prominent views of vertical circulation, bridges, and upper level perimeter walkways so visitors can see retail functions on the second and third levels.

18

EHDD's late 1970s design for a ski resort just west of Park City, Utah, resulted in Deer Valley, a complex of two day lodges: Snow Park Lodge, at the base of the slopes, and Silver Lake Lodge, at mid-mountain. The project was heavily influenced by the WPA lodges built by the National Park Service in the 1930s. The buildings seem to have always been part of the environment. Materials were chosen for their strength, beauty, or appropriateness, and the building forms were a direct response to the heavy snowfall. The lodges house a mixture of program spaces, from dining and lounge facilities to changing rooms and ticket sales areas. All of the functions are melded into a seamless rustic whole, nodding to the early Metcalf House of 1948.[19]

The Blackstar Brewery, in Whitefish, Montana, went from Esherick's conceptual sketch to a functional brewery in eight months. EHDD was very interested in the owner's desire to locate the facility in close proximity to the raw ingredients used in the brewing. The project's simple form is reminiscent of agrarian farm buildings in that region. The space housing the brewing equipment is an extraordinary, three-dimensional, Rube Goldberg–like construct that is visible from the exterior. Clad in painted metal siding with large expanses of steel sash windows, it glows bright in the cool Montana sky, allowing the public to see every step of the brewing process through its panes. Blackstar Brewery was the last commercial project designed by Esherick.

The Autobahn automobile dealership, like its predecessor, RAB Motors in San Rafael, California, is an icon and an advertisement, addressing the speed of the highway and the hi-tech nature of the Silicon Valley site in Belmont, California. Peter Dodge designed the building's gentle, arcing, aluminum-clad western façade to screen the outdoor sales areas from the wind and the sounds of the expressway. This façade gives the dealership a memorable stature when viewed by motorists traveling on the nearby expressway at 70 miles per hour. The building enclosure arcs vertically and follows the curve of the abutting on-ramp, the outer edge of the site. The auto showroom is seen from the freeway as a stage, framed by a large glazed opening in the metal façade, revealing new cars under the spotlight. Daylight is carefully controlled by a series of horizontal sun shades on the west-facing glass along the freeway; warm, soft light emanates from the nylon fabric canopies covering the outdoor sales and service areas on the east side.

19

20

18 Silver Lake Lodge, Deer Valley Resort,
Park City, UT, 1981
Photographer: Peter Aaron/ESTO
19 Blackstar Brewery, Whitefish, MT, 1995
Photographer: Roger Wade
20 Autobahn Motors, Belmont, CA, 1996
Photographer: Peter Aaron/ESTO
21 BART Station, Walnut Creek, CA, 1973
Photographer: Wayne Thom
22 Offices of the Secretary of State
and the California State Archives,
Sacramento, CA, 1995
Photographer: Mark Citret

PUBLIC PROJECTS

In the 1970s, EHDD was selected to design two stations for the Bay Area Rapid Transit division of Cal Trans (in association with Gwathmey, Sellier and Crosby). The firm's contract was later expanded to include five more stations east of Oakland, in Contra Costa County. The architects were responsible for designing the structures, humanizing the spaces, and creating smooth pedestrian circulation from the station entrances to the train platforms. The heavy concrete braces at the Walnut Creek station lend a self-assured and aerodynamic quality to the structure that suits its function.

The multi-layered Offices of the Secretary of State, in Sacramento, California, is the gem of the Capitol Mall district, attracting building tenants and visitors alike and offering a respite from the heat and the city streets. The rather workaday aesthetic of the perimeter block contrasts the drama of the courtyard. In her oral history, Reiss states that Esherick likened the experience of the complex to cutting into a watermelon; there is a revelation of the sharp contrasts between inside and out.[20]

In the late 1980s, the State of California commissioned EHDD to plan and design the Offices of the Secretary of State and the California State Archives complex. The project site occupies a full city block in the Capitol Mall district of Sacramento. This is a multi-use facility complete with museum, archives, storage and research spaces, an auditorium, office space, and parking facilities. The complex gives the appearance of several smaller structures, so as not to overtake the scale of the neighborhood. As in the Cannery and McPhee Union projects, the design directs visitors through an outdoor public courtyard as they make their way towards internal spaces. Indigenous materials were used throughout and, as in the Union, bright colors enliven the public spaces and make reference to the ubiquitous California poppy.

AQUARIA

EHDD's aquarium projects began in 1966 with the design of a commercial attraction across the street from the Cannery, commissioned by the same client, Leonard Martin. The Penguinarium project was a response to the growing tourist trade in the Fisherman's Wharf area. A group of behavioral scientists at the University of California, Los Angeles, supported by Martin, had offered their expertise in the training and study of penguins for research purposes.

18

The Penguinarium was open for nearly a year but quickly suc-cumbed to a changing real estate and tourist market. However, it gave EHDD its initial exposure to exhibit design and the technical aspects of marine exhibit tanks. Unfortunately, no photographs of the completed project remain.

In the early 1970s, Jack Wagstaff of UC Santa Cruz again approached Esherick with a commission to help the university design a small marine lab on the Pacific coast just north of Santa Cruz. Esherick, always up to the challenge of delving into new and idiosyncratic assignments, eagerly took on the job and worked with Chuck Davis and UC scientists to develop a facility for the study of marine mammals and inter-tidal research. The Coastal Marine Laboratory is a farm-like compound of sheds and tanks, reminiscent of the legendary Doc Rickets' lab from Steinbeck's *Cannery Row*. This project exposed EHDD to the myriad of technical challenges in marine research facilities, which include acquiring process water, stabilizing water temperatures, preventing algae growth, and designing structurally sound tanks, complicated filtration systems, husbandry service areas, and small labs. The laboratory proved to be invaluable experience.

23

A few years later, EHDD had become, under the leadership of Chuck Davis, the only West Coast architectural firm qualified to design a world class aquarium financed by hi-tech pioneer David Packard of Hewlett-Packard. What would eventually become the Monterey Bay Aquarium was conceived as a public, non-profit

teaching and learning attraction that would fund an independent marine research facility to study the vast ecosystems of Monterey Bay. The success of this facility, and the resulting tendencies for municipalities to build aquariums to revitalize depressed urban waterfronts, has led EHDD to implement master plans and designs for new aquariums both nationally and internationally.

24

(1) Jacques Leslie, "A Gold Medal for Understatement," The New York Times, March 2, 1989.
(2) Peter Dodge, Architecture California, July/August 1986, p.25.
(3) Marc Treib, " William Wilson Wurster: The Feeling of Function," An Everyday Modernism: The Houses of William Wurster, San Francisco Museum of Modern Art/University of California Press, 1995, pp.16-17.
(4) Joseph Esherick, An Architectural Practice in the San Francisco Bay Area, 1938-1996, Vol. 1, Regional Oral History Office, The Bancroft Library, University of California, 1996, p. 172.
(5) Joseph Esherick, "Joseph Esherick: Theory and Practice," Western Architect and Engineer, December 1961, pp.20-37.
(6) William Wilson Wurster, "The Twentieth-Century Architect," Architecture: a Profession and a Career, AIA Press, Washington, D.C., 1945.
(7) Robert Venturi, Quote from a written endorsement to the AIA of EHDD for the firm of the year award, 1986.
(8) Frank D. Welch, "Life Work: The Architecture of Joseph Esherick," Texas Architect, 9/10, 1994.
(9) David Gebhard, "William Wurster and His California Contemporaries: The Idea of Regionalism and Soft Modernism," An Everyday Modernism: The Houses of William Wurster, San Francisco Museum of Modern Art/University of California Press, 1995, pp.164-180.
(10) Esherick, An Architectural Practice in the San Francisco Bay Area, 1938-1996, Vol. 1, p.162.
(11) Esherick, An Architectural Practice in the San Francisco Bay Area, 1938-1996, Vol. 1, p.164.
(12) Ken Tadashi Oshima, "The Modern House in the Postwar Period, Part 6: Grounding Modernism for Everyday Life: Goldman House by Joseph Esherick," a+u: architecture + urbanism, Feb. 1998, pp. 126-133.
(13) Joseph Esherick, "Form is What Things Are," Progressive Architecture, May 1964, p.137.
(14) Esherick, An Architectural Practice in the San Francisco Bay Area, 1938-1996, Vol. 2, p.472.
(15) Charles Moore and Gerald Allen, "Two Buildings by Joseph Esherick: Dedicated to the Moving Inhabitant, Not the Maker of Form," Dimensions: Space, Shape & Scale in Architecture, Architectural Record Books, 1976, p.76.
(16) Donald Canty, "Sea Ranch: Original Development," Progressive Architecture, Feb. 1993, p.87.
(17) Esherick, An Architectural Practice in the San Francisco Bay Area, 1938-1996, Vol. 2, p.378.
(18) Moore and Allen, pp.71-76.
(19) Charles K. Gandee, "Uphill, Downhill: Deer Valley Resort, Park City, Utah," Architectural Record, May, 1983, pp. 92-97.
(20) Esherick, An Architectural Practice in the San Francisco Bay Area, 1938-1996, Vol. 2, pp.614-615.

FEATURE PROJECTS

MONTEREY BAY AQUARIUM
MAIN BUILDING
OUTER BAY WING
MONTEREY, CALIFORNIA (1984, 1996)

On the dramatic Northern California coast, EHDD designed one of the most successful and widely acknowledged aquariums in the world, the Monterey Bay Aquarium. Conceived as a public non-profit educational facility, the completed aquarium, which also houses an independent marine research institute, is the result of a collaborative effort between the aquarium's marine biologists and the architectural team. In an important departure from traditional aquarium design, the Monterey Bay Aquarium focuses on the unique marine ecology of one habitat: the Monterey Bay and its shoreline. Rather than being locked into a single path through the building, the visitor is presented with many options for exploring at leisure, heading to a single exhibit, or touring the building from top to bottom. The facility provides a passive education for small groups of visitors and a formal education for the school children who attend the aquarium's focused programs each year.

The aquarium sits sensitively among the existing ramshackle sardine processing plants and old cannery buildings, utilizing the foundations—and rekindling the spirit—of the old Hovden Cannery that was left in disrepair after the decline in the canning business in Monterey. The designers chose materials that harmonize with the existing fabric and withstand the damp weather that rushes in from the Pacific Ocean. The concrete frame aquarium is crowned with a wood truss structure that recalls the qualities of factory construction and a roof covered with concrete tiles to withstand the elements. The architects kept the boilerhouse and the pumphouse as part of the aquarium complex to tell the story of the canning industry in the new building.

The building sits half over the water and half on the land, participating with the environment that it examines. Unlike other aquariums, the Monterey Bay Aquarium makes a strong connection with the outdoors rather than enclosing its exhibits inside a black box environment. Large expanses of glass offer the visitor scenic views of the bay. The architects also established a lively outdoor terrace, where visitors can peer at the seals perched on nearby rocks, catch a glimpse of the annual migrating whales, and gaze into the tidal basin.

Inside, the first set of galleries occupies approximately four acres. This area focuses on the diverse marine habitats of the nearshore waters of the Monterey Bay and includes more than 80 habitat tanks, exhibiting 5,500 specimens from nearly 400 species. Some of the most spectacular habitats are constructed in a series of massive acrylic-enclosed tanks. A towering giant-kelp forest cultivated in a three-story tank with 335,000 gallons of seawater marks the first time kelp was grown in a captive environment. Computer sensors monitor the life-support functions of each tank. The combined raw and filtered seawater system allows nutrient-rich seawater to be brought into the system or water clarity to be increased for better viewing of the exhibits. Another huge tank inhabited by sharks, bat rays, and other indigenous fish has sandy sea floors, barnacle-encrusted wharf pilings, and deep reefs typically found in Monterey Bay.

One of the aquarium's most popular attractions is its 55,000-gallon sea otter exhibit. Many of the endangered sea otters come from the kelp forests off the coast of Monterey, and the aquarium not only serves as a home for several of these animals but also provides vital research and rescue facilities for the otters. Visitors can see these marine animals move from their rocky coastal habitat above the water to their underwater environment. Other galleries and exhibits show the coastal stream and the rocky shoreline habitats

of the underwater wildlife, as well as an aviary filled with shorebirds.

Significant technical innovations were achieved in the aquarium's design. Water drawn directly from the bay provides the exhibits with an infusion of nourishing natural organisms during evening hours; during viewing hours, the water is filtered for more clarity. The water in the Kelp Tank is kept in constant motion; without this agitation, the kelp would be unable to extract the nutrients needed for survival. The building temperature is controlled by a heat-exchange system that uses the bay's water for cooling. Other tanks have devices to simulate waves lapping against the shoreline. A master console monitors the water quality of each tank and the performance of its filtering system. In the event of an emergency, such as an oil spill, the water intake system can be shut off and the tanks can operate independently for two weeks.

In 1996, 12 years after its initial work, EHDD completed a 90,000-square-foot addition to the east side of the aquarium. The Outer Bay Wing focuses on the habitats and species of the bay's outer, deeper waters, in particular on the muscular, stream-lined swimmers built for speed and long distance travel, and the gelatinous, soft-bodied drifters that move with the currents. The centerpiece exhibit of the new wing—a tank for sharks and schooling fish—is viewed through an immense, single-paneled acrylic window and holds an impressive one million gallons of seawater. In adjacent galleries, carefully lit tanks display the graceful movements of a vast range of jellyfish. The entrance to the wing boasts an innovative elliptical tank embedded in the ceiling, in which 3,000 glittering anchovies swim in a mesmerizing, never-ending circle.

23

With a large outdoor terrace around the tidal basin, the building, unlike black box aquariums, actively relates to the outside and the natural environment of Monterey Bay (facing page, top). The aquarium sits half on water, half on land, blurring the boundaries between controlled and natural environments (facing page, bottom). Siting the aquarium over the bay presented the design team with unique challenges such as maintaining public access and safety, and protecting the building from damp weather and wave run-up brought on by storms (below, top). The building embraces the bay and the tidal pool becomes a public theater (below, bottom left). Both phases are sensitive to the industrial aesthetic of Cannery Row, yet also function as a state-of-the-art aquarium (below, bottom right).

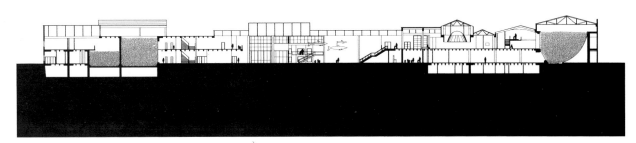

Longitudinal section

Life-support and mechanical systems were left exposed to maintain an industrial aesthetic in the Marine Mammal Hall. The layout of these systems was carefully planned by the design team to facilitate the movement of air and water through the building, and to suggest the speed of the great cetaceans gliding overhead **(facing page, top)**. The Kelp Tank houses the first giant-kelp forest to survive under artificial conditions. The tank is three stories tall and contains 335,000 gallons of seawater **(facing page, bottom)**.

The boiler house from the former Hovden Cannery was retained as a feature of the ticketing lobby **(below, top left)**. The two-story Main Entry Hall is the nexus of the aquarium and orients the visitor to Monterey Bay immediately upon arrival **(below, top right)**. The Dunes and Marshes exhibit is a covered exterior space presenting views, smells, and sounds of the sea **(bottom, left and center)**. A vertical public staircase allows views to the outdoors and orients visitors in the aquarium **(bottom, right)**.

The Kelp Tank is center stage when divers perform feeding demonstrations in the kelp forest (**above, top left**). Acrylic bubble windows allow visitors to "enter" the tanks for views of marine life not possible through conventional tank windows (**above, top right**). Tall tank windows express the soaring heights of the kelp forest swaying in the current (**above, bottom left**). Two-level viewing of the Kelp Tank (**above, bottom right**). Night view of the Main Entry Hall from the outdoor terrace (**facing page**).

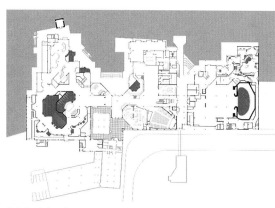

Main level plan ⊕

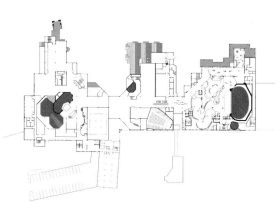

Second level plan

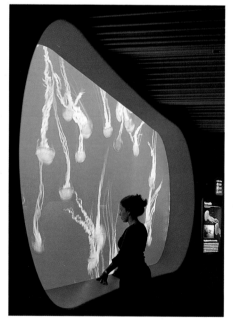

The Cannery Row elevation conforms to the scale of the historic street while providing the necessary service access for a world-class aquarium **(above, top)**. The aquarium provides free access to the Monterey Bay for the general public **(above, bottom left)**. A custom-designed tank allows the public to see the mesmerizing pelagic jellyfish in their open water habitat **(above, bottom center)**. The extension of the Main Entry Hall to the east links Phase One of the aquarium to the new Outer Bay Wing **(above, bottom right)**. The module and massing rhythms of Phase One were extended into the Outer Bay Wing **(facing page, top)**. The Outer Bay tank holds 1.1 million gallons of seawater and is viewed through one of the world's largest single acrylic windows **(facing page, bottom)**.

UNIVERSITY OF CALIFORNIA
LIBRARY & CENTER FOR KNOWLEDGE MANAGEMENT
UC SAN FRANCISCO (1990)

The UCSF Library & Center for Knowledge Management, completed in 1990, was the first of many academic library commissions awarded to EHDD and was pivotal in developing the firm's expertise and reputation in the field of academic library design.

Located on UCSF's Parnassus campus, the 120,000-square-foot library sits near the base of Mt. Sutro on a steeply sloping site with panoramic views of the city, the Golden Gate Bridge, and the Marin Headlands. The architects designed the building to complement the built environment of the campus and the surrounding residential community with sensitively scaled forms constructed of glass fiber–reinforced concrete, limestone, glass, and metal in a modern version of the San Francisco Bay Area vernacular. Set into the natural grade of the site, the library steps down the hill as it completes the northwestern edge of the campus.

The library contains one of the country's largest health sciences collections, used annually by over 650,000 visitors, including researchers from the biomedical and pharmaceutical industries, students, and faculty. The building's design will accommodate 20 years of expansion by allowing for lesser-used reference materials to be transferred to compact shelving. The building is fully wired for technology and its flexible design will accommodate future computer and telecommunications technologies.

Comfortable services, collections, study, and staff spaces support operational efficiency. Large expanses of glass bring light into the interior spaces, and a variety of reading nooks and rooms—some integrated into the stacks, some located at the perimeter of the building—provide individual and group study space and offer spectacular panoramic views.

The library's collections are housed on five floors. Visitors enter the building at the campus street level through the third-floor lobby, where the circulation and reference desks are located. This floor contains the more frequently used portions of the collection: reference, documents, and current periodicals, as well as a 24-hour reading room. The lower two floors are utilitarian in nature, housing the majority of the older bound periodicals, classrooms and training rooms, the non-print collection, the interlibrary loan department, staff work spaces, and library administration. The fourth and fifth floors are more elegant, featuring beautifully paneled conference and reading rooms, and a Japanese garden on the fifth floor terrace. These floors contain monographs; an extensive, museum-quality collection of art; rare books on the history of medicine and Asian medicine; and medical instruments and other objects relating to the health sciences.

The library's top three floors function like an art museum and are equipped with appropriate environmental controls, display lighting, and security systems. In recent years the library has mounted major exhibitions of its own collection as well as the works of artists such as Rodin and Isamu Noguchi.

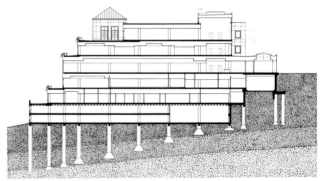

North-south section

The library's large building area is more apparent on the north side which steps down to greet the residential community below **(facing page, top)**. The fifth floor terrace features a Japanese garden and panoramic views of the city, the Golden Gate Bridge, and the Marin Headlands **(facing page, bottom)**.

Although the building is quite large, at 120,000 square feet, its stepped nature does not overpower the small residential buildings surrounding it **(above, top)**. The architects chose glass fiber–reinforced concrete, limestone, glass, and metal for the exterior of the building **(above, bottom left)**.

Site plan ⊕

First level plan

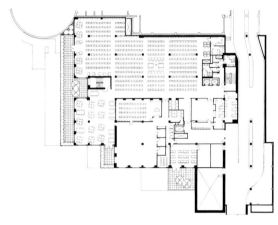

Second level plan

Street level plan

Fourth level plan

Fifth level plan

To the south, a modest three-story façade
meets the street (facing page, top). The
entrance canopy physically extends the building to the street (facing page, bottom).

Reading rooms on the upper floors are elegantly appointed. The Browsing Room houses a non-medical collection and is used primarily for relaxation **(facing page, top)**. The reading rooms on the fourth and fifth floors provide sweeping views of the San Francisco Bay and Marin County **(facing page, bottom)**. Large windows in the Asian Collection reading room minimize the need for artificial lighting during daytime hours, and show a sparkling cityscape after dark **(this page)**.

UNIVERSITY OF CALIFORNIA
SCIENCE LIBRARY
UC SANTA CRUZ (1991)

The Science Library is located atop Science Hill on the UC Santa Cruz campus, near existing labs, classrooms, and offices. The beautiful but challenging site was markedly sloped and covered by mature redwoods. EHDD felt it was imperative to create a design that minimized the number of mature Douglas fir and redwood trees removed, to preserve the feel of the grove from inside and outside the building.

The entrance to the library, which is set into the hillside, is located at the middle of its three levels. The architects integrated a large terraced plaza to create a focus for the adjacent science buildings. Bridges are threaded among the trees, connecting the entrance to the upper plaza and the surrounding buildings. The trees, which are visible from all levels, filter the hot summer sun and allow for extensive use of glass throughout the building. A sawtooth plan and staggered shelving layout integrate reader space near every volume, without sacrificing efficiency or requiring the removal of trees from the site.

The library's exterior is clad in board-formed concrete with vertical resawn boards. Copper shingles, which were used on the exterior of the building as an infill material, enliven the building's subtle palette.

The architects chose concrete as the structural system throughout because of its increased seismic resistance in shear walls. A waffle slab system was selected for its strong two-way load distribution, and fewer columns maximize the flexibility of organizing library shelving.

Inside the library, the architects exposed the structural waffle slabs and board-formed concrete at the wall surfaces. Clear maple tongue-and-groove boards accent the concrete walls in certain spaces, including the periodical reading room. Circulation and reference desks are constructed of maple casework with granite tops. Perimeter spaces are devoted to treehouse-like reading areas. The 280,000-volume capacity of the library can be increased to over 350,000 volumes by converting to compact shelving, without changing the structure, lighting, air conditioning, or furnishings.

The library incorporates state-of-the-art data and communications systems, including on-line catalogs and an electronic collection area with 50 workstations supplemented by outlets for laptop computers in the group study rooms. General collection areas also encourage users to plug in their own computers to access catalog and collection data throughout the nine-campus University of California system.

The long, sloping entryway is a bridge leading up to the entry on the second of three floors **(facing page, top)**. Clad in board-formed concrete with vertical resawn boards, the library's exterior presents an abundance of windows and strong vertical lines, which help the building fit nicely into the thick grove of trees **(facing page, bottom)**. The large terrace at the library's entrance centralizes all activity in the cluster of science buildings **(above)**.

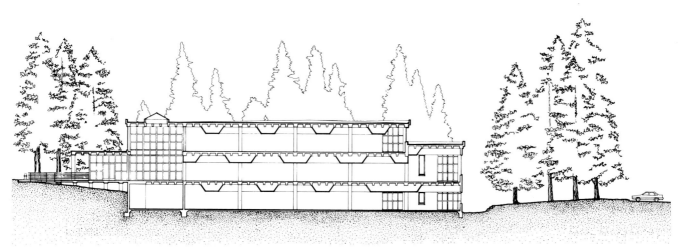

Section

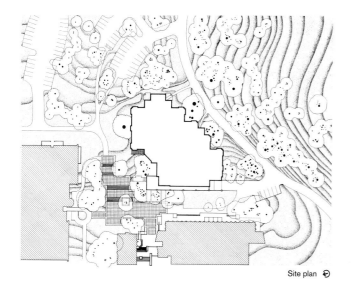

Site plan ⊕

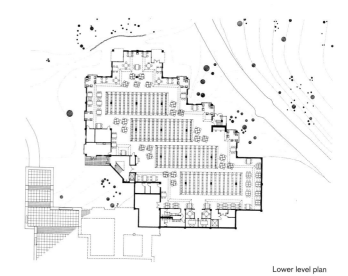

Lower level plan

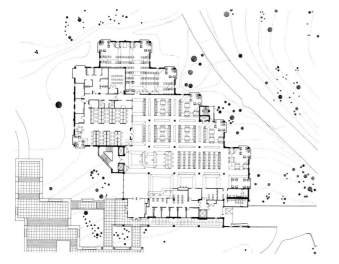

Main level plan

Upper level plan

Large windows lend the reading rooms a tree-house-like feel **(below, left)**. Exposed board-formed concrete and structural waffle slabs on the building's interior articulate its modern, almost industrial feel, appropriate for a science library **(below, right)**. Located on the middle of the library's three levels, the double-height lobby gives a feeling of grandeur to the project **(facing page, top)**. The vast vertical expanses of glass at the entrance allow visitors to appreciate the scale of the redwoods surrounding the building **(facing page, bottom)**.

44

UNIVERSITY OF CALIFORNIA
MAIN LIBRARY COMPLEX
UC BERKELEY (1995)

In 1986, the Main Library complex at UC Berkeley consisted of three major buildings, located at the center of the campus. Doe Library, designed by John Galen Howard and completed in 1912, housed the 1.2 million-volume central collection of arts and humanities, and a number of other major collections. Its Beaux-Arts north reading room and north façade are in the National Register of Historic Places. Bancroft Library, designed by the office of Bakewell and Brown and built in 1949 as an addition to Doe, houses many special historic collections. The third building, Moffitt Undergraduate Library, is a separate modernist building located downhill from Doe and built partially into the hillside.

EHDD's renovation of the Main Library complex comprised the first phase of a master plan. Included in this were the seismic strengthening of Doe and Moffitt Libraries, preservation of the historic character of Doe, removal of the main collection from the unsafe central core area of Doe, and provision of a modern stack facility of 180,000 square feet for an expanded two million volumes.

The project presented a number of opportunities. Faced with the challenge of fitting the proposed addition into a sensitive site next to an historic structure, EHDD opted to create a largely underground structure to the north of Doe. The design team was thereby able to fulfill an early campus plan by John Galen Howard that created a large open space in the center of campus, around which buildings would be clustered. By concealing the underground addition and moving a cross-campus road to the north edge of the new open space, the architects succeeded in restoring Howard's central glade.

The need both to respect the historic façade of Doe and to provide accessibility presented another challenge. EHDD discovered from old renderings that Howard's original design had included an elaborate granite terrace to the north, facing the central glade, which

was never built. The architects resolved to complete Howard's design by relocating existing historic granite steps 25 feet to the north and creating a new classical terrace around them. Meanwhile, by contouring the landscape on the roof of the addition, the firm was able to make the main north door wheelchair accessible.

After studying the longitudinal section through the site, including Moffitt Library, the architects realized that it was possible to link Moffitt Library to Doe Library via an underground addition. EHDD's plan combined the entire physical plant of the complex into one structure, providing greatly improved flexibility for overall library space planning and moving the receiving dock away from the campus' landmark campanile.

After deciding to place the addition underground, the firm was confronted by librarians and users with an entirely new set of concerns. Foremost among their needs was keeping the plan organization simple and understandable so that the layout of the vast collection would be perceived easily by users and would provide a sense of openness and security. A second objective, as prescribed by the librarians, was to mitigate the sense of being underground.

The architects solved the first concern by creating a large atrium space with a staircase that delivers patrons to a broad aisle serving the entire stack area on each floor and celebrates the vertical circulation. Likewise, in a reference to the Beaux-Arts approach of Doe Library, EHDD designed a series of large rooms on the uppermost level, which are linked on a major axis and connected by short intervening spaces.

The designers achieved their second objective—to produce light that is comfortable and relatively glare-free, which was more difficult—with a variety of skylights and openings between levels. The firm looked to three masters who understood daylighting in libraries—Gunnar Asplund and Alvar Aalto—for inspiration and techniques to achieve these qualities.

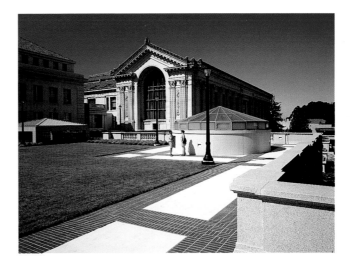

A top priority in this project was to preserve the historical façade of Doe Library, pictured here. The architects relocated the historic granite steps and created a new classical terrace around them (facing page, top). Original steps were moved farther from the building to implement John Galen Howard's plans for a previously unrealized terrace. This new terrace provides accessibility to the main entry and forms the roof structure over the stacks below (facing page, bottom). The architects chose to build the addition underground, creating the new central glade, and linking the buildings in the library complex both below and above ground (right). The library complex comprises several buildings, from left the famous campanile, the Bancroft Library, and Doe Library (this page, bottom).

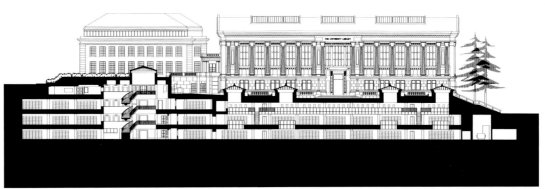

East-west section

The second level reading room is circumscribed with a band of ash panels doubling as the guard rail for the mezzanine above (facing page, top). As seen from the mezzanine reading room, a series of balconies and light wells maintain a sense of openness underground, and give students a variety of work and study areas (facing page, bottom).

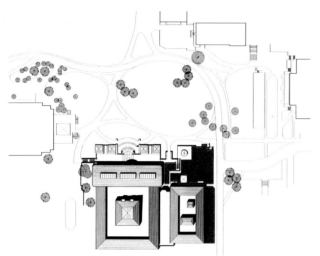

Site plan ⬆

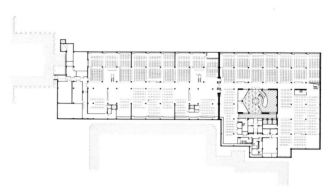

First level plan

Mezzanine level plan

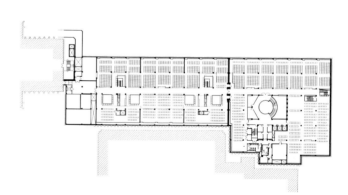

Second level plan

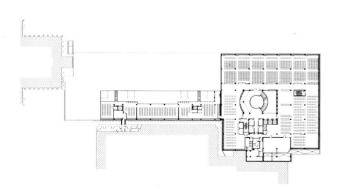

Third level plan

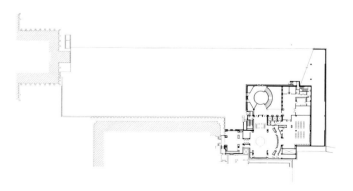

Fourth level plan

50

The atrium stairway, the library's centerpiece, provides access to all levels of the facility **(above)**. The lighting design and ash panels for the underground library space were inspired by many great architects, such as Alvar Aalto and Gunnar Asplund **(below left and right)**. The grand spiral staircase in the atrium cuts through all levels of the building, centering activity and creating a strong sense of circulation in the library **(facing page)**.

JOHN G. SHEDD AQUARIUM
FACILITY MASTER PLAN
CHICAGO, ILLINOIS (1996)

Chicago's John G. Shedd Aquarium has been a venerated institution and a major lakefront landmark since it opened in 1930. Its visibility from Lake Michigan and Lakeshore Drive, as well as its powerful termination of Roosevelt Road, establish a presence rivaled by no other institution in the city. In 1996, EHDD, in collaboration with Perkins & Will, developed a master plan that addresses the aquarium's growth into the next century and its place in the aquarium industry; analyzes its high volume of visitors; emphasizes the importance of the historic building (which precluded obscuring any of its façades); and proposes respectful reinterpretations of the building's scale, materials, and ornament.

In 1997, Go Overboard!, the Shedd's latest gift store, opened with larger-than-life murals and sea creatures, creating an underwater atmosphere. Two years later, the Caribbean Reef opened in the Shedd's central rotunda. The exhibition, which added a new multimedia display to a refurbished reef tank, was also a chance to restore the rotunda's architecture to its original splendor. In 2000, Amazon Rising, an exhibit that takes visitors through the annual South American rain cycle, opened in the historic galleries south of the rotunda.

In 2003, visitors will witness the opening of a subterranean addition to the Shedd's south flank, which will present Ocean Kingdoms, a compelling story about coral reefs living off the Philippine coast. The exhibit's highlight is a 400,000-gallon tank showcasing the interface of the reef, the ocean, and pelagic sharks. The addition reveres the original 1930s structure by cleverly extending the terrace of the historic Shedd to form a multipurpose outdoor area over the new exhibit. Aquatic motifs are celebrated in the addition's details without slavish replication of the original ornament, clearly identifying it as a contemporary building.

In addition to these exhibits, the architects are renovating the Shedd's entrances to accommodate the boost in visitors that the new exhibits are expected to bring. To the south, a new bus and vehicular turn-around/drop-off will accommodate the aquarium's need for a strong identity and provide access from Solidarity Drive, the main artery connecting the Shedd, the Field Museum, and the Adler Planetarium. New landscaping on the Shedd's south side will also help integrate it with this recently completed Museum Campus.

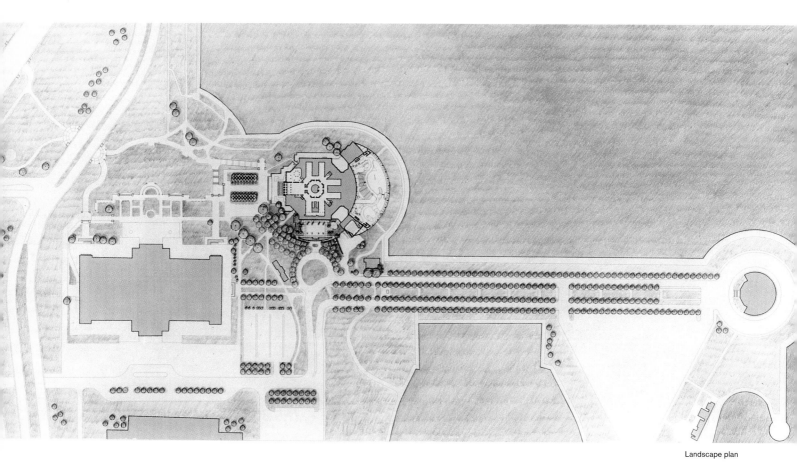

Landscape plan

West elevation

South elevation

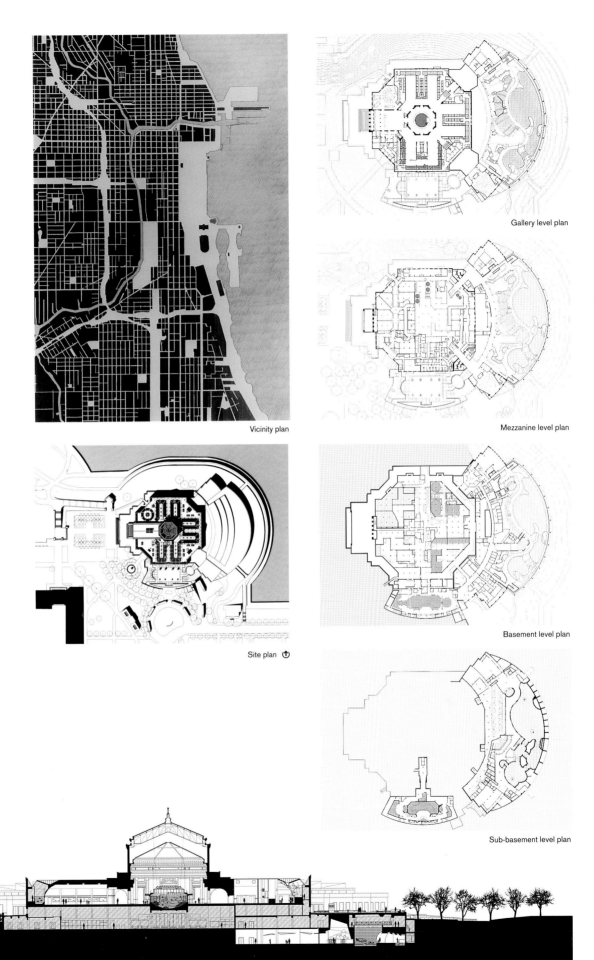

Vicinity plan

Gallery level plan

Mezzanine level plan

Site plan ⌖

Basement level plan

Sub-basement level plan

North-south section

JOHN G. SHEDD AQUARIUM
GO OVERBOARD!
CHICAGO, ILLINOIS (1997)

The John G. Shedd Aquarium promotes the enjoyment, appreciation, and effective conservation of aquatic life and its environment through education, research, and public display. Go Overboard!, the Aquarium's in-house shop, continues that mission by helping guests learn about the natural world with merchandise related to the aquatic environment and an exciting, fun, and extraordinary retail experience. EHDD and Schwartz Architects developed the underwater atmosphere of Go Overboard! with varied materials and colors, carpeting with a wave-like design, theatrical lighting, multiple video screens, surround-sound speakers, and enlarged photo-murals that cover the store's perimeter walls.

The expanded and renovated store occupies 6,000 square feet in the northwest quadrant of the historic Shedd Aquarium. The shop's centerpiece is a mammoth, cable-suspended fiberglass octopus spanning 28 feet across, with eight tentacles wrapping around eight structural columns in a spiraling embrace. Six cameras projecting aquatic video images onto the octopus create the illusion of water movement. The creature's eyes are twin TV monitors that morph images of other species' eyes in a constantly evolving sequence that culminates in the human eye.

The store's fixtures and five thematic departments—Coral Reef, Rain Forest, Shedd Architecture, Kids, and Books—radiate from the great looming octopus. Super-realistic fiberglass aquatic creatures are perched atop sandblasted glass shelves mounted on custom, seaweed green–stained plywood fixtures. The ten creatures are approximately four feet high, with some as long as eight feet, and include a cleaner shrimp, seahorse, leopard shark, red-eyed tree frog, sea turtle, triggerfish, moray eel, porcupinefish, rock iguana, and rockhopper penguin. The aquatic imagery of seven curving, vibrant, ink-jet printed on vinyl photo-murals continues the underwater theme.

The architects selected evocative text, laser-cut and applied to wall friezes, to define individual sales areas. The book department, for example, targets adults and uses a quote from Shakespeare: "One touch of nature makes the whole world kin." Each freestanding book fixture supports large etched and tinted acrylic panels containing engraved images and excerpts from the works of Melville's *Moby Dick*, Stevenson's *Treasure Island*, and Verne's *20,000 Leagues Under the Sea*. The architecture department features a mural with an enlarged copy of a 1927 blueprint of the historic Shedd building. The Coral Reef department's fixtures feature large, abstract coral formations in overlapping eight-foot-high laser-cut iridescent pink acrylic. A giant photo-mural of a coral reef looms over a rear bank of built-in wall shelves.

flamingos. A sw... ... An army of frog

Oceanic Seahorse
...NCHES (3-10 CM)

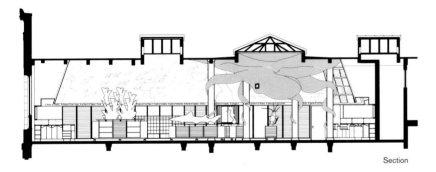

Section

The centerpiece of the store, a cable-suspended fiberglass octopus, spans 28 feet across, its eight tentacles wrapping around the store's structural columns (**facing page, top**). A great variety of sea creatures gives visitors reason to continue their exploration beyond the museum and into the store (**facing page, bottom**). View between the porcupine fish and moray eel to the Rainforest and Coral Reef–themed areas (**above, top left**). The octopus' eyes are actually video monitors that display the eyes of many different species in an evolving sequence that culminates in the human eye (**above, top right**). Multiple video screens display constantly changing video images (**above, bottom left**). Enlarged photo-murals cover the store's perimeter walls (**above, bottom center**). The book department supports large etched and tinted acrylic panels featuring engraved images and quotes from various books about the sea (**above, bottom right**).

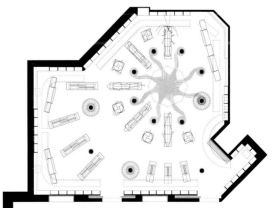

Plan ⟳

JOHN G. SHEDD AQUARIUM
CARIBBEAN REEF EXHIBIT
CHICAGO, ILLINOIS (1999)

Once the brightest space in the Shedd Aquarium, the 5,800-square-foot central rotunda originally housed a small swamp exhibit illuminated by daylight streaming in through translucent laylite 65 feet above the floor. An alteration made in 1970 introduced a 90,000-gallon coral reef tank into the hall, which necessitated the elimination of all daylight in favor of a dark, controlled environment. That renovation destroyed the historic laylite and wall surfaces, which were painted black and dark green, and made the once-bright rotunda the Shedd's darkest space.

While the reef tank had been drained and renovated twice since 1970, no attempts were made to restore the architectural space to its original splendor. EHDD, working in collaboration with Perkins & Will, identified the rotunda as the first exhibit space to be completed as part of their comprehensive facility master plan for the Shedd. The design team, working in conjunction with the Shedd's Department of Planning and Design and John Vinci, historical architect and principal of the Chicago-based firm Vinci/Hamp, began work on the space in 1997. Many of the rotunda's original 1930s details were restored, and the reef tank, the largest marine tank within the historic aquarium, was refurbished with a new habitat to underscore the connectivity between the aquatic environments of the earth.

The controlled-lighting environment necessary for the reef tank precluded daylight-only illumination in the rotunda because of its natural fluctuations, its contributions to algae growth, and potential reflections. A translucent material replaced the glass laylite panels. A blackout curtain above it shields the exhibit from sunlight. Interior illumination is accomplished with dimmable fluorescent fixtures above the laylite. Gelled, high-pressure sodium fixtures located above the blackout curtain bathe the original exterior skylight of the rotunda in an aquamarine glow.

The rotunda space was painted a brighter color to match the original paint used in 1930, and original nautical appointments such as the clock, nautilus torchieres, and fish-shaped sconces were restored. Acoustic panels, painted to match the walls, mitigate reverberation. In the future, the reef tank may be removed and the space returned to its original function as a central, daylit circulation space.

The reef tank's 70-year-old gravity-fed filtration system was replaced with a new high-pressure sand filtration and fractionation system. New HVAC equipment in the former gravity filter space replaced the 1970 system, which had been located in the interstitial area above the laylite.

The new exhibit is a theatrical experience within the building, combining nature and high-tech audio-visual effects. Regularly scheduled live dives take place in the tank. Volunteers tell the audience about the reef as they feed the animals in the tank. The lighting changes according to the events taking place in the rotunda. When there is no dive taking place, the laylite provides higher levels of general illumination to showcase the architectural detailing and the dramatic volume of the space. Before a dive takes place, lights dim and projected quotations about sustainability, awareness of the environment, and appreciation of the earth appear on the rotunda's walls and laylite, theatrically transforming the space. During the dive, the house lights dim to focus attention on the tank, its interpretive graphics, and on sounds and images from real-time plasma video screens and a new audio system.

Wenn wir versuchen,
etwas Eigenständiges
zu finden, erkennen
wir, dass es mit allen
anderen Dingen im
[...]

Quando tentiamo
di distinguere
una cosa
dal suo insieme,
troviamo che tutto
nell'*universo*
è collegato.

- John Muir, 1911

The lighting above the ceiling's translucent laylite panels is easily controllable; the light can be dimmed significantly if a dive is taking place in the tank, or brightly lit, making the rotunda the brightest room in the aquarium. Quotes from naturalists and environmentalists are projected in the space, emphasizing the connectedness of people and the environ-ment **(facing page)**. EHDD restored much of the detailing on the walls, including the shell-shaped skate sconces **(above, left)**. Along with the nautilus torchieres and historic benches, the designers also restored the finishes and paint colors to their original 1930s state **(above right)**.

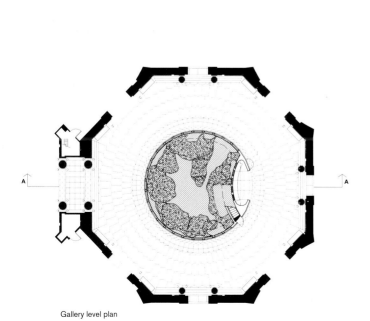

Gallery level plan

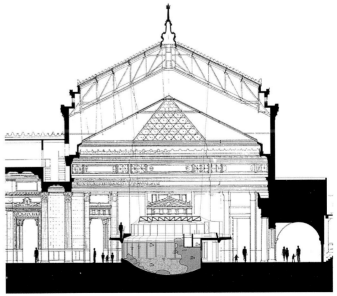

East-west section

JOHN G. SHEDD AQUARIUM
AMAZON RISING EXHIBIT
CHICAGO, ILLINOIS (2000)

Amazon Rising is the third major renovation to Chicago's historic John G. Shedd Aquarium since 1997. Completed in June 2000, the Amazon exhibit is part of an $85 million facility master plan developed in 1995 and scheduled for implementation over the next ten years. The original 1930 Beaux-Arts building, with its Greek Cross plan, was designed as a series of six isolated galleries radiating from a central rotunda—the classically appointed hub of the aquarium renovated by EHDD in collaboration with Perkins & Will.

Amazon Rising reorganizes 16,000 square feet of existing galleries and support spaces to the south of the rotunda into a unique exhibit that leads visitors on a path charting the seasonal ebb and flood of the Amazon River, beginning with the dry season and the story of human habitation in the region. Traditional wet habitats coupled with interactive, multimedia technology create a fully immersive exhibit experience within the historic building.

EHDD, in collaboration with Perkins & Will, responded to the Shedd Department of Planning and Design's program with an architectural approach that is complementary to the exhibit storyline and peels back the layers of time to reveal spaces and structures of the old building never before seen by the public.

Two former classic galleries and a former animal husbandry area, reserved for aquarium support equipment and reserve tanks, were combined into three contiguous galleries that wrap around a core of support and circulation space. The exhibits are integrated with the architecture, immersing visitors in the Amazon River environment of exotic plants and animals. In the first and third galleries, the small glass windows of traditional specimen tanks were removed and replaced with large floor-to-ceiling acrylic panels,

providing wider views into the tanks and admitting more light into spaces that had previously been too dark for viewing. The second, or transverse, gallery depicts a flooded forest and an aboriginal dwelling. The closing gallery presents the economic and cultural impacts of the river's seasonal flooding.

Although the habitats are seamlessly connected throughout the galleries to conform to the exhibition's storyline, the architectural environment changes dramatically throughout to balance the programmatic needs of the exhibit. The design plays against the salient features of the old building to create a contemporary space within a historic context. The transverse gallery, for instance, which showcases the flood season with large tanks, exploits the natural light abundant in a former service area by exposing the visitor to multiple skylights above. The original steel roof structure of this gallery was freed from its former concrete encasement, covered with a fire-protective coating, and left exposed. Its arcing forms and lacey, riveted construction recall Jules Verne imagery, while creating a conservatory-like atmosphere that sharply contrasts with the historic plaster details and artificially lit cylindrical vaults of the two historic galleries.

State-of-the-art life-support systems sustain several species of birds, reptiles, and mammals, including piranha, marmosets, an anaconda, and a caiman crocodile. An outdated gravity filtration system in a rooftop penthouse was replaced with an expanded mechanical penthouse to maintain the ventilation and high humidity requirements of the exhibit. New lighting, audio-visual systems, climate controls, and fogging devices were employed to simulate the tropical environment.

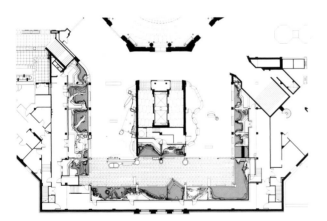

Gallery level plan

New steel and glass screen walls were inserted between historic galleries and the transverse gallery to create a physical and metaphoric change of atmosphere between thematic areas **(facing page)**. The designers replaced the small glass windows with floor-to-ceiling acrylic panels, admitting more light into the public space and providing wider vistas of the pre-monsoon season of the Amazon River **(above left)**. Visitors can feel water droplets from the rain wall created to herald the flood season **(above right)**.

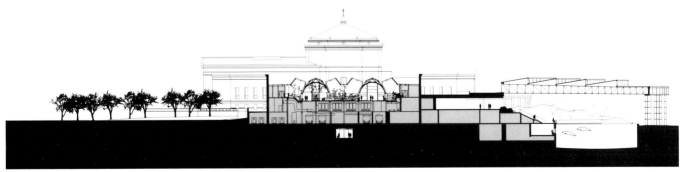

Cross section

68

AQUARIUM OF THE PACIFIC
LONG BEACH, CALIFORNIA (1998)

As the centerpiece of Long Beach's urban waterfront revitalization, the Aquarium of the Pacific adds a major public educational venue to the city's downtown area. The building anchors one end of the new Queensway Bay marina development, which replaced a run-down and underutilized waterfront park. The project will eventually include retail, restaurant, and office developments spurred on by the construction of the aquarium.

The aquarium exhibits the diverse life forms of the Pacific Ocean, with a focus on three distinct areas: the temperate waters of Baja California and the Gulf of California; the cold waters of the North Pacific in the Sea of Okhotsk; and the warm waters of the tropical South Pacific near Palau. The exhibit concept is open-ended, allowing future additions to focus on other areas of the Pacific without altering the overall theme. The exhibits are meant to inspire conservation and environmental awareness.

The City of Long Beach wanted a building that would become an icon on the new waterfront—a facility that would be educational as well as recreational to attract people to Long Beach from the greater Los Angeles area. In addition, the aquarium was to be a major civic center where events and gatherings could take place. The architects responded to this request and established a grand lobby space within the narrow site.

The main entrance is located on the north side of the site. The lobby funnels visitors through the full length of the building before beginning the exhibit tour. A series of "teaser" tanks on the ground floor draws visitors through the curving space, culminating in a large exhibit window "apse" at the end of the lobby. Clerestories above the lobby flood the space with natural light.

Once through the lobby, visitors exit the building and ascend a series of terraces that make up the outdoor Baja California exhibit on the sunny south side of the building. They are then drawn up to the second floor and back inside the building. The remaining exhibits occupy two interior exhibit loops on the second floor. The lobby space reorients the visitor after each loop.

The lobby also divides the wet side of the aquarium from the dry side. The wet side includes all of the exhibits, exhibit support spaces, and life-support areas that house pumps, filters, and other equipment. The architects constructed these spaces out of concrete to accommodate large quantities of seawater, which is both heavy and corrosive. Ducts and other metalwork are constructed of stainless steel to prevent corrosion. As a cost-saving strategy, the architects grouped functions that did not directly involve seawater, such as classrooms, auditorium, gift shop, and restaurant, together on the dry side and constructed them with light steel.

The architects used water as an important metaphor in the building's design. Its forms are sinuous and curved; there are few right angles or straight lines in the building. The roof is composed of soaring, curved forms, giving the building a recognizable identity from the marina and downtown Long Beach. The aquarium was the first building on the redesigned waterfront, and its nautical/oceanic motifs set the tone for the development that followed.

The designers chose aluminum for the roofs and window systems because it is cost-effective and resistant to corrosion, and cement plaster for most exterior wall surfaces because its malleable nature was conducive to curving forms. Interior materials include stone floors and plaster walls in the public areas, and carpeting (for acoustic purposes) in the exhibit areas. An aluminum slat ceiling in the lobby accentuates the curvature of the roof and hides mechanical equipment and acoustical insulation.

The western side of the site is devoted to services, including life-support equipment that can be placed outside in the temperate climate. The northern part of the site is reserved for future expansion. In addition to the exhibits, major public outdoor spaces include a restaurant and a large terrace between the aquarium and the lobby. Both spaces offer views of the downtown area and the famous ocean liner Queen Mary, another Long Beach attraction.

The lobby reorients visitors after each turn through the aquarium space (**facing page**). Comprising a series of curved forms, the roof suggests the motion of waves, giving the building a recognizable shape and identity from downtown (**this page, top**). The Baja California exhibit is an exterior portion of the exhibit path on the south side of the building (**this page, bottom**).

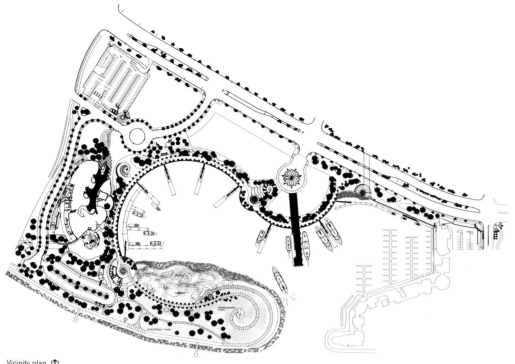

Vicinity plan ⊕

The main entrance to the aquarium as seen at dusk (facing page, top). The way the building undulates at the edge of the waterfront suggests the motion of waves (facing page, bottom).

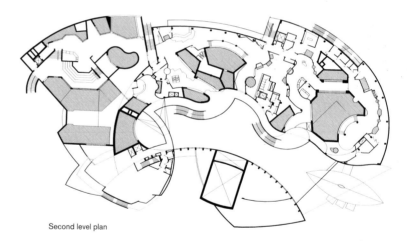

Second level plan

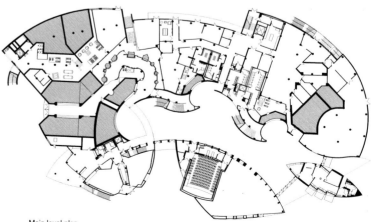

Main level plan

PUBLICIS & HAL RINEY HEADQUARTERS
SAN FRANCISCO, CALIFORNIA (1998)

The objective of this interior renovation for Hal Riney & Partners (now Publicis & Hal Riney), a leading international advertising agency, was to create a pleasant, inspiring work environment for the company's hip, 350-person San Francisco headquarters. The 120,000-square-foot office space is a three-story, triangular-shaped concrete building designed by Gensler & Associates in 1972 and located across from Fisherman's Wharf, with dramatic views of the San Francisco Bay along the Embarcadero and Telegraph Hill.

Because of the fast-track nature of the project—design and construction were completed in ten months—the client selected the contractor prior to choosing the architect. The contractor remained integrally involved in the project from the first interviews to final occupancy. The project was successfully completed within the extremely tight time frame because of the contractor's vigilance and the constant communication between architect and client. There were three main contacts at Hal Riney who were responsible for making all design decisions and two architects who worked very closely with the client throughout the entire process. Such a short chain of command made the decision-making process smoother and faster, while the client's decisive nature and the tight schedule helped quickly lock design concepts into place.

The client's request for a "loft-like" work environment was a driving factor in the design of the project. To achieve the airy, open quality the client sought, the architects relocated private offices to the center of the building and wrapped them in a custom system of anodized aluminum and clear plate glass, corrugated glass, and translucent glass to bring natural light into these offices. They increased the height of the space by removing the existing acoustical ceiling and exposing the mechanical, power, lighting, data, and sprinkler systems.

The architects also wanted to create a simple framework that would not compete with the chaotic working style of the client, so they called for sandblasted concrete walls and columns, and had the concrete ceiling and the majority of the walls painted white. They introduced color minimally yet dramatically: deep purple/blue on the elevator doors; red, yellow, and blue rubber flooring; large areas of blue, orange, and mustard wool carpet; and red, orange, green, and blue partitions. All of the materials combined to create a series of textures and colors that shifts between rough and smooth, neutral and intense.

EHDD worked directly with Vitra to furnish the office floors, using Ad Hoc furniture and Memo storage units to create the most flexible office system possible. The pod layout, furnishings, and power connections allow users of the space to efficiently rearrange the work areas.

In addition to reconfiguring the floors, the architects also dramatically altered the character of the existing building by moving the entrance to the more prominent elevation along San Francisco's Embarcadero. This change created a more dramatic and inviting entry that takes advantage of an existing landscaped plaza on the Embarcadero.

The architects wanted to create an airy, loft-like feel to the space, which they achieved by leaving much of the office open, while enclosing private offices and conference areas in transparent or translucent glass **(above)**. The reception desk is complemented by red leather Le Corbusier lounge seating **(facing page)**.

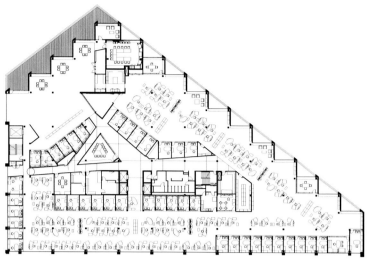

Third level plan

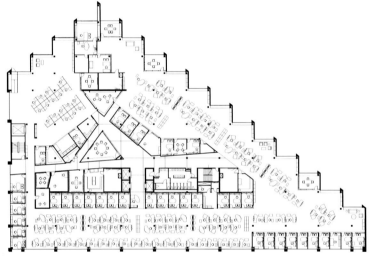

Second level plan

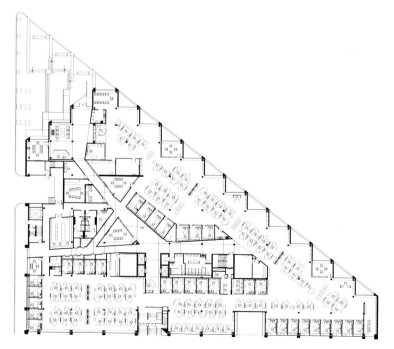

First level plan ⟳

By walling the conference rooms in translucent glass, the architect was able to bring a feeling of openness and light in the space while maintaining privacy within **(facing page, top)**. Conference rooms with windows have dramatic views of the Embarcadero and the San Francisco Bay **(facing page, bottom)**.

The openness of the various areas and flexibility of the office furniture allow the space to be easily reorganized and workers to be easily regrouped **(facing page, top)**. Exposed concrete column capitals and mechanical systems give the space more apparent height and accentuate the loft-like feel. Work areas are kept primarily open for a convivial environment **(facing page, bottom)**. Unusual shapes within the circulation corridors preserve spatial variety within the large floor plate **(this page)**.

81

Segments of the façade along Turk Street and
Van Ness Avenue are finished in glazed
ceramic tile showcasing students' artwork.

TENDERLOIN SCHOOL AND COMMUNITY CENTER
SAN FRANCISCO, CALIFORNIA (1998)

San Francisco's Tenderloin neighborhood is well known as a dangerous community that typically experiences more than 300 violent crimes each month. Yet it also has a long history of attracting people in transition and newcomers to the city, and has been a leading relocation spot for Southeast Asian families since the early 1980s.

A local advocacy group, the Bay Area Women's and Children's Center (BAWCC), helped make the public aware of the more than 1,000 children living in the Tenderloin, who, because there was no elementary school in the neighborhood, were being dispersed to some 47 different schools throughout the city. Joined by a persistent and dedicated community group and the strongly supportive San Francisco Unified School District, BAWCC increased its public awareness campaign, pushing for the establishment of an elementary school and community center in the Tenderloin. This effort ultimately led to the passage of Proposition A, a school bond measure authorizing funds to build the Tenderloin Community School. BAWCC also contributed money, allowing for an expanded program that would include a preschool, community center, and parking garage.

Joseph Esherick, EHDD's founding principal, was involved in the project at its outset. Before funding was secured, Esherick worked with BAWCC, community members, parents, children, teachers, and principals to define program requirements and articulate the vision for the project (donating all of his time and services). After the passage of Proposition A, the San Francisco Unified School District selected EHDD to design the school. The design team worked with community groups and the San Francisco Unified School District to select a site—which is located at the boundary of the Tenderloin and the Van Ness Avenue urban corridor—for issues of safety and visibility. The school will hopefully become a new "safe" symbol for the neighborhood.

Vivid amid the otherwise visually austere Civic Center area of San Francisco, the building's exterior is painted red and yellow, colors considered auspicious in various Asian communities. The architects designed the public face of the school, which runs along Van Ness Avenue, to provide space for art and banners designed by students. Some 5,000 glazed tiles, created by children from nearby Redding Elementary School and public artist Martha Heavenston, are mounted on the building's Turk Street and Van Ness façades.

With its diverse program, strong community influence and outreach, and physical design, the Tenderloin Community School challenges traditional notions of the school as a closed fortress. The building design makes efficient and creative use of space on a tight site, accommodating a number of resource centers that serve the schoolchildren and their families. These include a medical and dental clinic, counseling rooms, adult education classrooms, a parent resource center, a community kitchen, and a community garden, in addition to the elementary school.

The inclusion of three separate play yards, including two on the rooftop, was a design and programming priority since the children of the Tenderloin have little open space in which to play in their neighborhood. Parents and children also requested a community garden—an important element in numerous cultures.

Inside the building, the spatial layout integrates school and community functions and allows for maximum interaction between parents, students, teachers, and staff. The designers used color as an orientation device: different floors are identified by different colors. Each classroom was designed to include private spaces for learning and teaching. Bay windows along the Turk Street side of the building are reminiscent of the Bay Region style; inside, they provide small-scale "break-out" areas in the classrooms. The mechanical, structural, and telecommunications systems of the building were left exposed, establishing the building itself as a teaching and learning tool.

Vivid colors were chosen for the school's exterior, as can been seen on the Turk Street façade, to distinguish it as a vibrant icon for the neighborhood **(above, top)**. The library juts out into the courtyard, creating variety in the façade, and separating the ground-level play yard from the community garden **(above, bottom left)**. The taller space, containing the gymnasium, as seen from Van Ness Avenue **(above, bottom right)**. It was important to the designers to create a variety of play areas, as there is a lack of safe open space in the Tenderloin. The school, therefore, has three play yards, two of them on the building's roof **(facing page, top)**. The south courtyard remains a warm outdoor space most of the day **(facing page, bottom)**.

Joseph Esherick conceptual sketch

Section/south elevation

West/north elevation

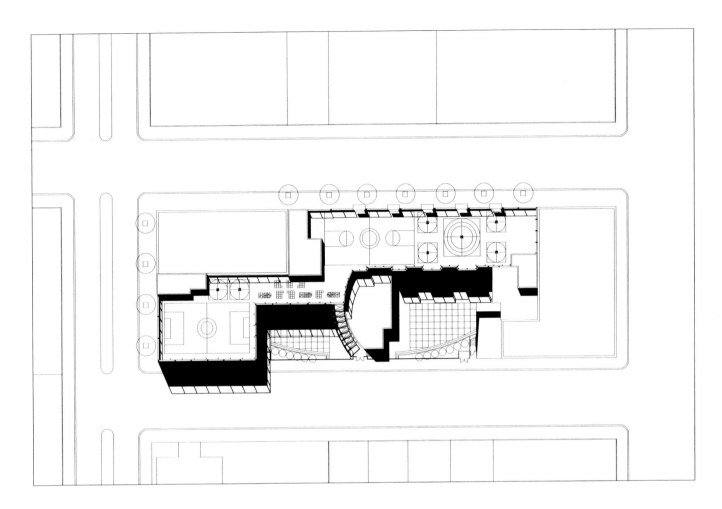

Site plan ↻

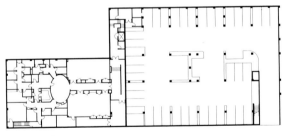

Lower level plan

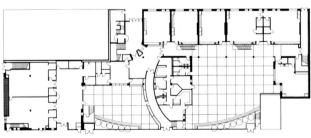

Main level plan

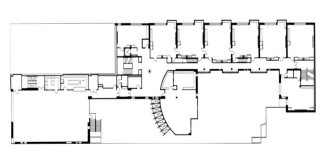

Second level plan

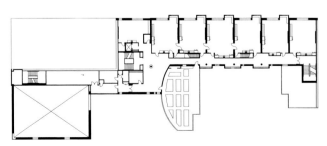

Third level plan

The library has many windows, but still feels cozy and has a child-like scale **(above)**. The double-height gymnasium is an area in which children can peacefully learn to play sports, distanced from the noise and activity of Turk Street and Van Ness Avenue **(below)**. Alcoves in the hallway have window seats, giving children varied space to read and meet quietly **(facing page, top)**. Bay windows, an integral component of Bay Area architecture, are provided in the classrooms as "break-out" areas, shown here to the instructor's right **(facing page, bottom)**.

EXPLORIS
RALEIGH, NORTH CAROLINA (1999)

Exploris is a dynamic children's museum in downtown Raleigh, North Carolina. The 70,000-square-foot brick structure fronts directly onto Moore Square, one of five historic parks planned for the city in the 1700s. The building design incorporates an existing 23,000-square-foot masonry warehouse that links the museum to Raleigh's historic streetscapes.

As the first interactive global learning center in the United States, with exhibits that feature on-line communication links to similar facilities around the world, Exploris encourages young people to explore, respect, and communicate with different cultures. Unlike many children's museums, which tend to be science- or health-based, Exploris focuses on people and their everyday experiences, using science and technology as a means of making human connections. The museum draws youths from ages eight to 14, from school districts across North Carolina and beyond.

The design team included EHDD and Clearspaces, a Raleigh practice composed of architects and an artist. The firms collaborated throughout the duration of the project and worked to blur the distinctions between art, architecture, and the exhibits. They sought to infuse the building with references to historic Raleigh and the surrounding region in order to expand and inform Exploris' educational themes of choice, change, interconnectedness, and perception. Sculptural and architectural elements in the entry courtyard allude to natural elements: sunlight, heat, rain, and wind. The Gate House, constructed of slats of southern yellow pine commonly used in 19th-century North Carolina barns, provides shelter for queuing visitors. Copper entry gates allow views into the courtyard and double as sound transmitters with brass mouthpieces into which visitors can speak to one another. The 50-foot-tall Wind Reeds installation, made of a composite material containing carbon fiber, generates the subtle sound of wind moving through tall grass.

One of the museum's most innovative architectural features is the World Wall, a three-story tall image of Earth as seen from space. Built of perforated steel panels containing 1.2 million glass marbles of varying shades, the World Wall is the exterior skin of the museum's black box exhibit space. The translucent colors of the marbles are brought to life at night by metal halide light fixtures.

Driven by the need for flexibility, the design team established several different types of exhibit spaces with contrasting architectural environments. "Human" exhibit spaces have a variety of ceiling heights and daylighting. "Green" exhibit spaces, located within a daylit area connecting two exterior courtyards, support plant growth and wet exhibits. The "black box" space supports tall exhibits and has a raised access floor, which provides maximum technical flexibility.

All of the exhibit areas come together in the museum's Global Space, the heart of Exploris that acts as the central reorientation space for visitors and accommodates large group gatherings, games, and performances. The red brick Global Wall, which forms the eastern edge of this space, grounds the building to its site metaphorically and provides a neutral backdrop. Overhead, an ethereal ceiling allows a natural balance of daylight at all hours of the day, reducing the need for artificial illumination.

Exploris resulted from a six-year collaboration among the design team, the owner/operator, and users. The goal was to design a building that would fit into historic downtown Raleigh but that would also have certain architectural features that clearly set it apart from the other buildings in the community. These features, such as the Look-in/Look-out Window—a cone-shaped aperture providing glimpses into and through the facility from Moore Square—and the World Wall, create a unique composition of building elements atypical of Raleigh. They push visitors to look again, ask questions, and walk away with an altered perception.

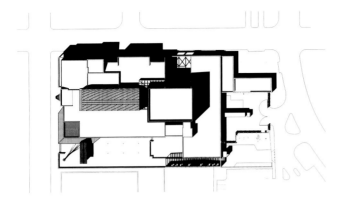

Site plan ⊕

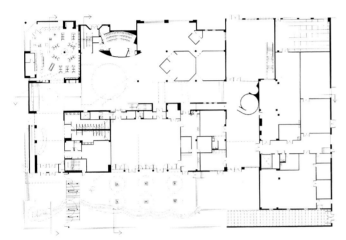

First level plan

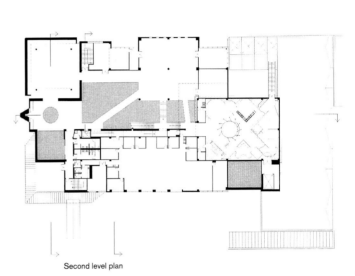

Second level plan

The Global Space represents the heart
of the museum. It acts as a central locator
and events space (facing page).

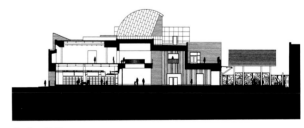

Section at lobby

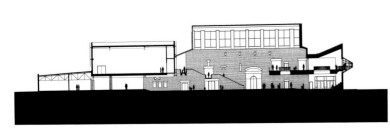

North/south section

East/west section at Global Space

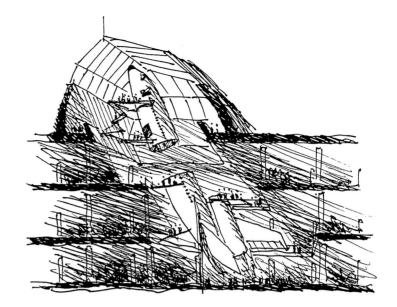

94

The entrance and east courtyard as seen from Moore Square at dusk. The wind reeds act as a marquee for the entry as they move with the breeze. The Look-in/Look-out Window allows views of Moore Square from within and views into Exploris from Hargett Street at night **(facing page, top)**. In keeping with the historic storefronts of downtown Raleigh, Exploristore has its own separate entry at the corner at Blount and Hargett Streets **(facing page, bottom)**.

Conceptual sketches of Global Space

At dusk, the silver of the World Wall's stainless steel panels slowly fades as the backlighting begins to illuminate the image of the earth from outer space **(facing page, top)**. The satellite image of the earth glows brightly against the night sky **(facing page, bottom)**. Detail of the perforated stainless steel panels supporting 1.2 million glass marbles in fifteen different colors **(this page)**.

97

EXPLORIS
EXPLORISTORE
RALEIGH, NORTH CAROLINA (1999)

Exploristore's fixtures and appointments were conceived as a neutral backdrop that would support merchandise from around the globe and allow the customers themselves to bring variety to the ambiance. The murals overhead connect conceptually to the exhibits in Exploris, and the overhead armature defines the ceiling plane and is used to support graphic signage.

Exploristore, the museum's gift shop, occupies 3,000 square feet of storefront space facing Moore Square. Entrances inside Exploris and on the street encourage museum visitors and passers-by to shop. The museum emphatically steered the design team away from a themed retail experience. Instead, the client insisted the store needed to connect conceptually with Exploris' educational mission through design, graphics, and carefully selected merchandise. The team responded with a flexible, neutral design that incorporates some murals related to the museum's exhibits, yet allows the merchandise to stand out. The store expresses the museum's mission and can also adapt to an evolving program.

The store is divided into three primary areas: "sales," for general merchandise; "gallery display," a more intimate area for higher-end merchandise; and "cash wrap," where sales transactions and gift wrapping services are carried out. There is also space for administrative functions and storage behind the cash wrap area. A secondary program requirement called for the inclusion of a small coffee counter, designed to attract people from the street and increase the amount of time the store's customers spend in the shop.

The sales area is outfitted with flexible merchandise display units and perimeter shelves supporting a slatted-wall display system. The brightly colored gypsum wallboard modules in the gallery display and cash wrap areas accent the white walls. Like the museum's exhibit areas, the ceiling was left open and all exposed mechanical systems were painted a dark green. Suspended below the display lighting is a sculpted steel armature that defines a ceiling plane and can support graphics and signage.

Overhead photo-murals wrap the sales areas with images of people, artifacts, and rituals from different cultures. Rendered in duotone, these murals reinforce the link between the store and museum while providing a neutral container for the customers and merchandise.

A rolling door fabricated of wood, perforated steel, and glass marbles provides access from the museum into the store. This door is reminiscent of a Chinese Moon Gate—an aperture from one space to another, through which light can penetrate. When open, it creates an important interior vista from within the museum.

A small coffee bar has been added on the street side of the store to draw customers from the outside and to entice visitors to linger **(facing page)**. The concentric circle pattern in the steel armature symbolizes unity and connectedness. The ceiling is left open above to enlarge the space and to make edges appear less defined **(above)**. Detail of the Gallery Display area intended for more expensive merchandise **(right)**.

BROOKFIELD ZOO
HABITAT AFRICA!—THE FOREST
BROOKFIELD, ILLINOIS (2000)

This addition to the Brookfield Zoo is a 9,500-square-foot structure housing an African rain forest exhibit with associated animal husbandry and service areas. Interior and exterior exhibits feature several rare okapi, blue- and yellow-back duikers, caimen, and Congo buffalo, as well as touracos and pea fowl, the forest's exotic birds. The exhibit story focuses on the sustainability of natural resources in the Ituri Rain Forest, located in the heart of Central Africa's Congo River area.

The new building is sited in an area of thick vegetation, designed to simulate the Ituri rain forest. In summer, the primary exhibit is outdoors; in winter, the exterior exhibit path is shortened and the primary attractions are featured within the 4,000-square-foot interior exhibit area.

The building is broken into three components, which help articulate the building's mass and give a visual hierarchy to the three basic program elements: the public exhibit, the okapi holding barn, and the general holding/building service area. In plan, the Z-shaped service building sits between the exhibit pavilion and the okapi barn. The plan shifts subtly off of the orthogonal to accommodate existing specimen trees and break up the otherwise rigid geometry.

The service building has a flat roof and is clad in a neutral, split-face concrete block. Attached to this utilitarian structure are the okapi holding barn and the exhibit pavilion. Both are taller wood frame structures with sloping, shingle-faced walls. The loftier okapi barn is designed for the comfort, care, and breeding of this rare animal. In the exhibit pavilion, the largest of the three components, a simulated path through the Ituri offers selected views of the animals in their habitats.

The program called for a modest background building that would not compete with its natural surroundings. To meet the budgetary and climatic requirements, asphalt shingles were chosen as the primary cladding material on the wood frame walls. They are a durable and time-tested Midwestern material used to protect modestly scaled buildings from the weather. In addition, asphalt shingles offer color variations and texture to cloak the building in a natural camouflage. On the exhibit pavilion and okapi barn, the shingles were applied in a custom, variegated pattern that enables the building to meld with the brown and green of the site's foliage, while adding much needed color to the site in the winter. The tilted, shingled wall planes render the building abstract and enable it to disappear behind the foliage of the rain forest, just as an okapi's markings help it blend with its surroundings.

Like the elusive okapi housed within, the exhibit building's variegated asphalt shingles lend color to the site during the Midwestern winter **(above)**, and help the building blend into the surroundings during the summer **(facing page)**.

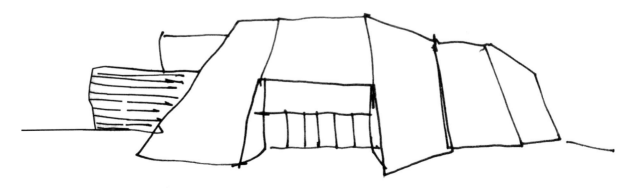

Conceptual sketch

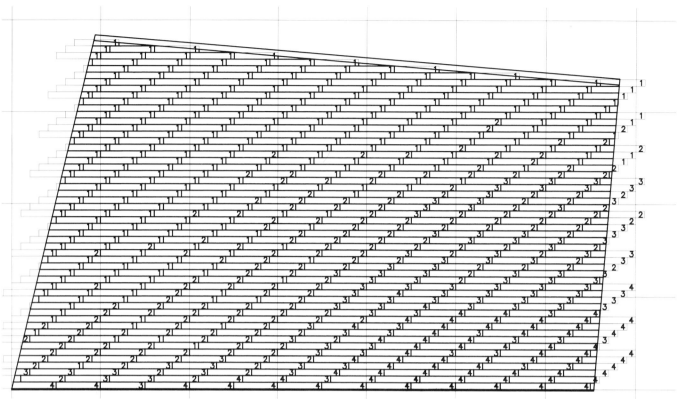

Shingle layout diagram

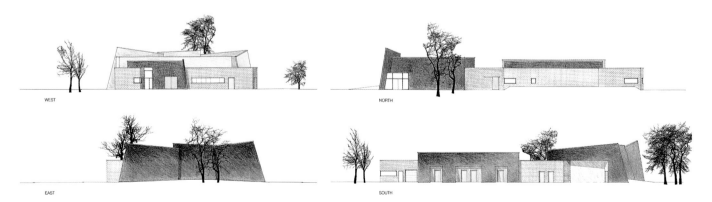

WEST

NORTH

EAST

SOUTH

Conceptual elevation drawings

Site plan ↻

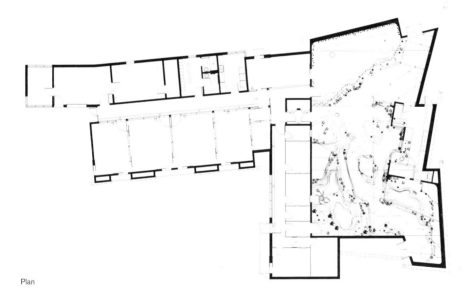

Plan

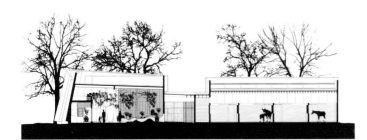

Longitudinal section

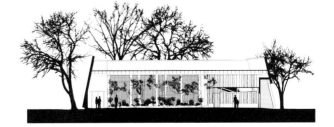

Cross section

The okapi barn is specifically designed for the comfort, care, and breeding of this rare animal **(this page, top)**. The large okapi stalls contain swing gates to allow keepers to separate males from females and females from their young. Non-toxic materials had to be specified because the okapi tend to ingest their surroundings **(this page, bottom)**.

The exhibit space focuses on the sustainability of natural resources in Central Africa's Ituri Rain Forest **(facing page, top)**. The indoor exhibit is the primary experience during the winter. Sun tubes admit natural light, simulating the dappled sunbeams of the rain forest **(facing page, bottom)**.

1001 Emerson exemplifies environmentally
sustainable architecture in both materials and
construction.

1001 EMERSON
PALO ALTO, CALIFORNIA (2000)

1001 Emerson is a home in Palo Alto, California. The owner, who is committed to the concept of environmentally responsive architecture, conceived of the project as a demonstration of how "green" principles could be incorporated affordably into everyday building practices, without sacrificing the design aesthetic. The house illustrates readily available construction alternatives that have a lower impact on the environment in terms of energy and water consumption, pollution, and the use of hazardous materials.

From the project's inception, the design team, consisting of EHDD architects, Drew Maran Construction/Design of Palo Alto, and the client, worked closely to realize these goals. Because the process began so early, the team was able to integrate sustainable materials and systems, such as photovoltaic panels, greywater collection, cellulose insulation, and low-e glass, into the design with only a five percent increase in costs. The team also was able to address site selection from a green perspective, choosing a site within walking distance from downtown Palo Alto to minimize the owner's reliance on an automobile.

The idea of a bridge was central to the design. The site is at the edge of an older residential community, in a neighborhood that marks the transition between auto repair and towing shops and a higher density retail, office, and residential district. The house has two wings linked by a transparent bridge and entry element. The bedroom wing is oriented on the city's linear street grid, while the living/master suite wing is rotated to face due south for maximum solar gain.

The owner wanted a simple plan, with primary space devoted to a large community room where all the basic functions of social and family life would occur. This space, used for cooking, eating, working, living, and entertaining, needed to be a virtual extension of the garden. Each family member also required individual, private space. These choices allowed for a smaller floor plan and a more communal environment for the client and her family.

Roughly 95 percent of the demolition materials from the site's previous building (an auto body shop) were recycled or salvaged. Some of this material was used in the new building, along with material from other remodeled homes. Construction waste (including concrete forms) was also recycled. Recycled glass tiles were used in the bathrooms and as exposed aggregate in the exterior concrete. The structural design minimized the amount of lumber needed, and an accredited Forest Stewardship Council certifier certified the framing lumber. All the wood used in the house was either certifiably harvested or engineered in a sustainable fashion, or recycled.

West-facing windows and exterior doors are glazed with Milgard Suncoat to reduce heat loads in the summer while maintaining 70 percent of daylight. Natural light is maximized by the home's orientation and by thoughtful placement of windows, thereby reducing the need for artificial lighting. Non-toxic and low VOC content glues, paints, stains, and floor finishes were specified to maintain a healthy quality of indoor air. Energy-efficient in-floor radiant heating minimizes fuel consumption. Cooling is through natural ventilation and temperature-sensitive exhaust fans. The entry, with a water sculpture and operable windows, acts as a cooling tower. West-facing exterior walls support steel vine trellises that act as vertical sunshades.

A full recycling center was built into the kitchen to make recycling as effortless as possible. A simple, structured wiring system allows for total flexibility within the house and supports high-speed access to the Internet. The system also provides for future improvements to the data delivery channels.

The bridge in the middle of the house was a central element of the design, linking the bedroom wing to the living/master suite wing **(above)**. Each of the house's two wings is on its own axis, adding to the complex geometry of the house **(facing page, top)**. The south wing of the house is shifted to a north-south axis to take full advantage of solar gain. The overhangs on the south side protect the dwelling from unwanted solar gain during the summer months **(facing page, bottom)**.

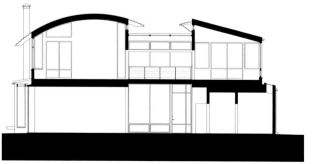

Longitudinal section

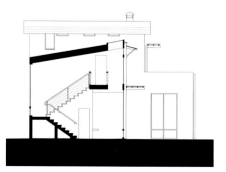

Cross section

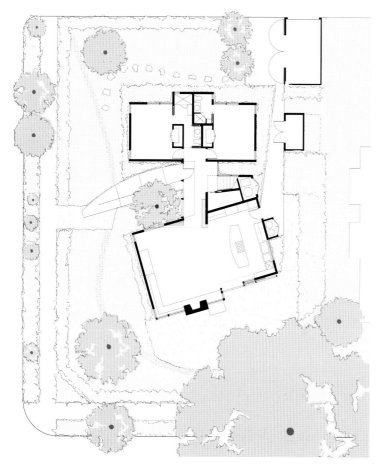

Site plan ⊕

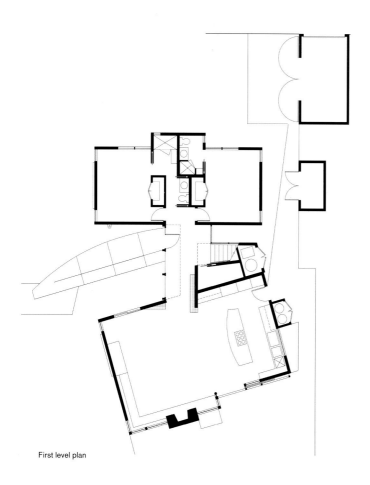

First level plan

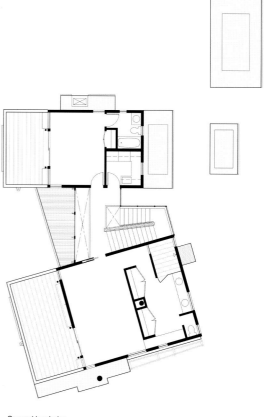

Second level plan

Steel vine trellises act as vertical sunshades,
cutting down on heat gain and helping
the client minimize energy costs (above).

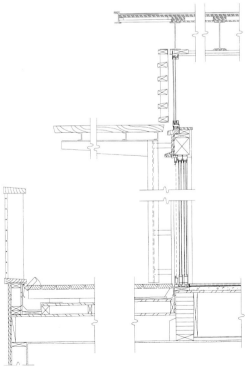

Detail section

116

The entry's operable windows and water sculpture help it act as a cooling tower for the building (above left). View of the entry space looking toward the community room (above right). The living room has large windows which maximize daylight and mini-

mize the need for artificial lighting (facing page, top). The master bedroom's windows are glazed with a coating which reduces heat loads in the summer while maintaining 70 percent of daylight (facing page, bottom).

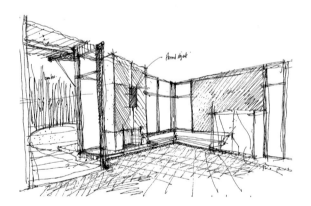

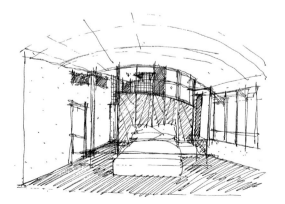

Conceptual sketches

Imagery for much of the structure, including the entry canopy, was taken from the natural forms of ocean waves and sea creatures.

THE NATIONAL MUSEUM
OF MARINE BIOLOGY/AQUARIUM
KENTING NATIONAL PARK
TAIWAN, R.O.C. (2000)

The Taiwan National Museum of Marine Biology/Aquarium sits at the northern entrance to Kenting National Park, located on the southern tip of Taiwan, facing the Taiwan Strait. The site originally comprised a black coral beach, ponds and support buildings, modest masonry dwellings, hemp fields, a small cemetery, and a coast guard station. Badly damaged as a result of hemp and aqua-culture farming during World War II, the site was restored with indigenous plant life that can survive the harsh, subtropical climate.

In their initial submittals for this project, EHDD's architects focused on traditions and images from Chinese culture. But it quickly became quite clear that the issues to be resolved at the site were those of function and climate, and that the facility, by its very form and use of materials, should evoke and convey the essence of the sea and the surroundings. They placed a priority on construction methods and materials common to Taiwan, such as cast-in-place concrete, stone, and ceramic tile.

Completed in 2000, the aquarium's first phase houses over 50,000 square feet of exhibits highlighting the waters of Taiwan. The remaining 150,000 square feet comprise a restaurant, gift shop, administration and education wing, mechanical space, and life-support space (where mechanical systems that keep the animals alive are housed). A second phase, completed in 2001, features a coral reef and marine mammal pavilion.

The building is a natural form nestled into the landscape and in harmony with the sea. A long, serpentine retaining wall encloses the entry plaza and shields it from the wind, and also reinforces the building's strong connection to the land. Because the site is vulnerable to typhoons during most of the year, inundation poses a constant threat. All public space is located above a plinth housing the life-support and mechanical spaces, which are equipped with sea doors to prevent flooding. The building's heavy structure is designed to resist typhoons and earthquakes and to keep the building fully operational during strong storms.

The architecture is at once western and eastern, with forms that read clearly from the coastal road without dominating the landscape. The public spaces and exhibit areas support wave-like roof structures that suggest the rise of the ocean swell and the forms of the great cetaceans displayed within. As a counterpoint to these large public areas, the administration, education, and gift shop wings are smaller, flat-roofed annexes that balance the building's composition. An important functional and aesthetic aspect of the design is a large arrival plaza, which serves as a ticketing venue. Beyond the ticketing booths is the entry court, which creates a smooth transition from outside to inside and provides a vital relief space for the crowds moving in and out of the building. In addition, the museum's entry canopy can be used as a stage for large-scale public events at night when the building is not in use.

The building's low, natural form harmonizes with both land and sea. A long seawall protects the building from typhoons and tsunamis **(above)**. The entrance side of the museum/aquarium has a water feature where whale sculptures frolic, enticing visitors into the shallow pool **(facing page)**.

Site plan ⏻

Conceptual sketch

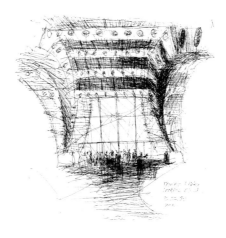

Conceptual sketches of entry/lobby

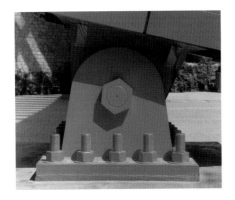

The museum's entry canopy protects visitors from the elements and celebrates the water theme when water pours from its overflow spouts during rainstorms (facing page, top). The lobby on the terrace that faces the Taiwan Strait glows at dusk (facing page, bottom). Canopy connection detail (this page, left).

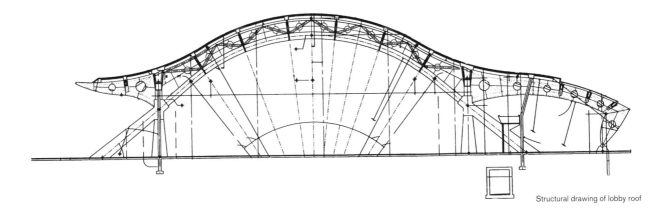

Structural drawing of lobby roof

Structural buttresses at the terrace anchor
the roof to the earth while evoking the ribcage
of a beached cetacean **(this page)**. The
heavy structure is designed to resist the many
natural forces prevalent on this exposed site:
severe corrosion, earthquakes, drop mountain
winds, typhoons, and tsunamis **(facing page)**.

124

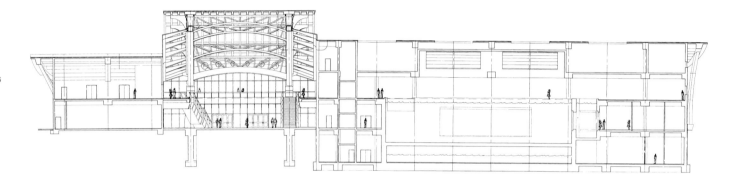

Longitudinal section

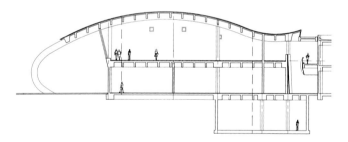

Section at temporary exhibit

East elevation

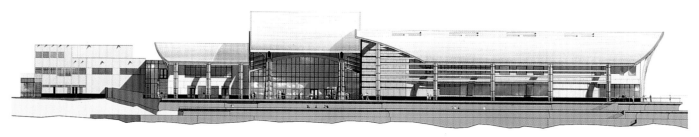

West elevation

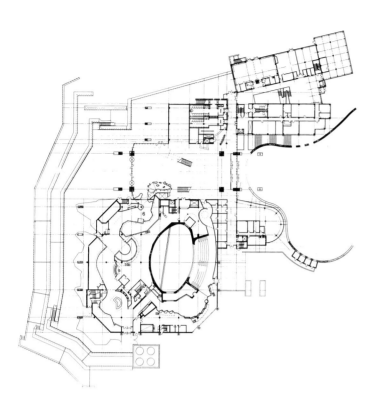

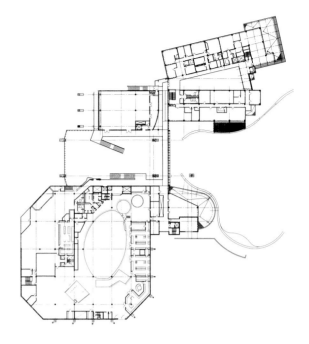

First level plan

Second level plan

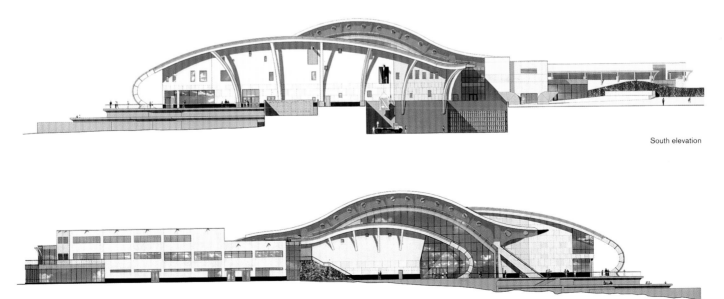

South elevation

North elevation

The lobby abounds with sea life native to Taiwan, and is composed of curving, organic shapes (this page, top). Clerestory windows define the joining of disparate building forms, washing the lobby with light and balancing the heavy glare off the Taiwan Strait (this page, bottom). The arcing form of the lobby's steel structure as viewed from the second level bridge. Steel is generally avoided in aquarium exhibit areas due to salt water corrosion but was used here to achieve the desired long spans (facing page).

View of the atrium at the administrative wing.
By creating multiple levels with bridges,
the architects maintained a sense of openness
in much of the structure **(facing page)**.
Lateral bracing at the buttresses is silhouetted
against the night sky **(this page)**.

131

CREATING THE EXPANDED SOLUTION

In a 1991 *Architectural Digest* interview, Joseph Esherick, one of the founders of Esherick Homsey Dodge & Davis, explained the firm's design philosophy: "Generally, my aim is to do things that are in some way indescribable and uncategorizable...[our] approach has remained much the same over the years and can be summed up with one word: listening. I believe that the basic approach to any project should be careful and ongoing attention to the client's concerns. The final result then becomes a knowledgeable and empathetic translation of those concerns and ideas. In one sense, there are no influences; in another, there are too many to name. The Austrian writer Robert Musil describes my dilemma eloquently: 'I am convinced that personal accomplishment means a hardly perceptible alteration of the spiritual riches which one receives from others, and...I believe this is true not only of what one attributes to the great traditions but also of what one takes in with every breath.'"

Esherick Homsey Dodge & Davis remains respectful of the early philosophies of the firm. The architects listen carefully to their clients, instead of being fueled by their own arcane rhetoric. They look to the client's own history and the history of the site, searching for those germane things that add meaning to the built form of a particular project, and adhere to Esherick's attitudes toward fit, context, and climate, always responding appropriately to a specific place. Having extended their practice into new

geographic regions outside California and, during the last decade, overseas, EHDD's architects also investigate regional attitudes as they relate to the program, local construction techniques, and local materials.

In 1997, the firm opened new offices in Monterey, California, and Chicago to serve its growing client base, offsetting the complacency that is often hard to overcome when continually designing and building in the same environment. The architects in the new offices have designed work that appears radically different from early projects, and their search for new terrain continues.

The design for the Indiana State Aquarium takes fit and appropriateness of materials to another level by grounding the building to the earth physically and metaphorically. The architects cast aside

1 American Conservatory Theater,
   conceptual sketch by Joseph Esherick,
   San Francisco, CA, 1990 (project)
2 The Archaeology of Now—
   A Museum of Recent History, Place Time
   and Symbol Competition Entry,
   First Place and People's Choice Award,
   Ottawa, Canada, 2000 (project)
3 Indiana State Aquarium,
   Indianapolis Zoo, 2001
4 Los Angeles Zoo Entry Plaza, 2002
5 EHDD Chicago Office, 1997
   Photographer: Doug Snower Photography
6 EHDD San Francisco Office, 1999
   Photographer: Peter Aaron/ESTO

MARC L'ITALIEN

proportion and refined form in favor of a more naturalistic building mass of undressed limestone blocks, the primary strata of Indiana, brought directly from the quarry—the inverse form of the quarry itself.

While the firm's architects share design philosophies, they do not pursue a standard style, instead generating different ideas and work with disparate clients who have particular demands. The firm thrives in these relationships, which bring uncertainty to the process and, ultimately, variety in the product. The firm's collaborative working process and its potential to yield unpredictable yet rewarding outcomes remains extremely important. Senior Design Principal Chuck Davis uses the term "expanded solution space" to describe the process of accommodating multiple voices in sometimes arduous working relationships with clients to produce unique design solutions. This attitude has led the firm to embrace a similar "space" within the studio itself. New voices, pluralistic thinking, and open attitudes strongly influence the final design solutions.

> EHDD has created "an inspiring organization and place to produce architecture, distinguished by modesty and sensitivity that practices great innovation and imagination through extraordinary empathy with context and site, and deep respect for craft, technology, client needs, public interest, and the planet."
> —AIA Statement, 1986 Firm of the Year Award

Today, large client groups have, for the most part, supplanted individual clients and are typically charged with representing the goals or mission of an institution. EHDD strives to embody these institutional goals in their projects leading, in the case of museums and aquariums, to designs that merge the exhibits with the architecture. EHDD has designed projects and landscapes that speak specifically to their content, while attracting the public. In some cases, such as Habitat Africa!—The Forest, EHDD streamlined this approach, designing the exhibits and habitats themselves and accentuating the cohesiveness between inside and out.

For a new entry to the Los Angeles Zoo, the architects coordinated the design of the landscape, outdoor exhibits, and the new

gate to emphasize the interdependence of plants, animals, and people in Los Angeles, as well as the zoo's early connections to the motion picture industry. The architecture alludes to the earlier Selig Zoo's historic gate with its monumental presence, and recalls the drama of a Hollywood world premiere with bold graphics and searchlights which pierce the night sky.

Although EHDD has grown in size and taken on larger projects, the firm still utilizes an internal team structure as opposed to departmental organization. Ideally the same team of architects follows a project from beginning to end to retain consistency throughout the job. The team designing the exterior of the building is also involved with the interior design, as they inform one another.

Though it is a large firm with multiple offices, EHDD is the antithesis of a corporate environment. The San Francisco and Chicago offices are arranged as open studios, devoid of partitions,

to encourage experimentation and the exchange of ideas. In San Francisco, studios for a staff of 70 are on two levels. The Chicago office is a small open storefront studio where 15 people work together. This office also experiments with projects and methods that are not always practical or financially feasible in the larger office.

Though it is committed to innovation, EHDD's traditions still run deep. Principals George Homsey and Peter Dodge remain heavily involved in the firm's culture. Both still produce construction drawings by hand in order to maintain a high level of quality and mentor

7

younger interns in the lost art of hand drawing. Some of the staff use only a mixture of two- and three-dimensional hand and electronic drawings, continuing Esherick's preference for designing with drawings as opposed to models, while others develop their projects in model form. In the absence of rigid standards, EHDD continues to employ a variety of design presentation techniques.

8

9   10

During the 1990s, EHDD's widely acclaimed aquariums and academic and public libraries, which expanded its client base outside California during this time, were becoming more influential than the firm's seminal early work. While Esherick was quick to admit that designing more than one of any new project type could present big challenges to the office, he was always eager to take on new project types. EHDD continues to pursue different building types according to the interests of the architects, who team up even before acquiring the commission to prepare proposals and project interviews with the client. This collaboration continues through construction and, finally, during promotion of the finished work. Solid designs, client referrals, and a reputation for meeting schedules and budgets have led to repeat work. For example, the pursuit and successful design of small laboratory renovation projects in the last ten years has yielded a growing portfolio of academic lab projects and has led to larger design-build lab projects for the University of California.

Private residential and academic student housing design continue to be cornerstones of the firm's work, although EHDD's internal goals have shifted somewhat. The Chicago office

11   12

recently won a City of Chicago–sponsored competition to build an environmentally sustainable case study house. Despite the Factor 10 House's modest size, scope, and budget, the project may have a far-reaching impact on housing in Chicago and, together with the 1001 Emerson house, on the firm's general reputation as a leading proponent of sustainable design. Common sense traditions, established with the Sea Ranch Hedgerow Houses of the 1960s, still drive the approach to current work.

The late architect James Stirling believed in visualizing and describing the central idea of a project through one single view—

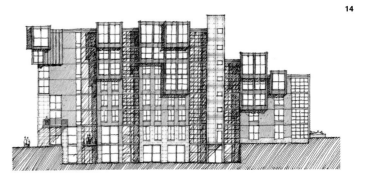

14

13

a vantage point that could illustrate his entire concept. While this is a useful way to present an unrealized project, EHDD finds this approach limiting. No singular image can fully describe their projects or the ideas represented therein. The Monterey Bay Aquarium, for instance, is profound for a variety of reasons: its close proximity to the bay, its prominent site at the foot of historic Cannery Row, the manmade tide-pool next to the sea, and the great Kelp Tank, which inspires awe in the viewer. Individually, these episodes tell only a fraction of the story; analyzing any single image prevents a true understanding of the total work. This perspective remains important to the firm.

Increasingly, EHDD competes for work and enters design competitions for the exercise and the challenge. Sometimes the project designers are acutely interested in the project type or the subject matter; sometimes they wish to promote a particular attitude or point of view, knowing the project may never be realized. In every case, EHDD devotes much thought to the particular problem at hand and emerges with specific ideas. The competition discourse further

stimulates and enriches the firm's design process as ideas generated during a competition might inform the design of other projects.

EHDD's employees have always been, and continue to be, part of an extended family. New staff members have the potential to be part of the organization for years to come and evolve with it. The firm's low turnover rate testifies to its conviction to developing staff. Perhaps the greatest reason so many stay at EHDD is the firm's inclusive attitude about the work. To go back to Esherick's quote of Robert Musil, EHDD seems to be enriched not only by ideas internal to the history, language, and practice of architecture, but also by the outside world, and the institutions and individuals

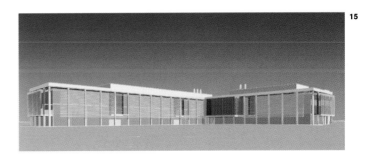

15

the firm serves. For Esherick Homsey Dodge & Davis, this presents a never-ending source of ideas, steering their work clear of cyclical architectural trends as they pursue instead the "expanded solution space."

CREDITS

MONTEREY BAY AQUARIUM MONTEREY, CALIFORNIA

ARCHITECT Esherick Homsey Dodge & Davis, San Francisco, CA

PRINCIPAL-IN-CHARGE Chuck Davis

PROJECT MANAGER Jim Hastings

ASSISTANT PROJECT MANAGERS Dan Chekene, Gilbert Scoggins

PROJECT TEAM Barry Baker, Larry Dodge, David Fagerstrom, John Haag, Kai Haag, Moritz Hauschild, Glenn Lym, Dennis Otero

GENERAL CONTRACTOR Rudolph and Sletten, Inc.

STRUCTURAL, CIVIL, AND LIFE-SUPPORT ENGINEER Rutherford & Chekene

MEP ENGINEER Syska and Hennessey

EXHIBIT DESIGN Richard Graef, Jim Peterson, Fredrick A. Usher

PROJECT MANAGEMENT Rhodes/Dahl

CLIENT Monterey Bay Aquarium Foundation

PHOTOGRAPHY Peter Aaron/ESTO: p. 21, 22, 23 (bottom left), 24, 25 (top, bottom right and left), p. 26 (bottom right), 27; Rob Lewine/Monterey Bay Aquarium: p. 25 (bottom center), 26 (top left); Monterey Bay Aquarium: p. 26 (top left); Kathleen Olson/Monterey Bay Aquarium: p. 23 (top), 26 (bottom left); Randy Wilder: p. 23 (bottom right)

MONTEREY BAY AQUARIUM OUTER BAY WING MONTEREY, CALIFORNIA

ARCHITECT Esherick Homsey Dodge & Davis, San Francisco, CA

PRINCIPAL-IN-CHARGE Chuck Davis

PROJECT MANAGER Scott Dennis, Jim Hastings

PROJECT TEAM Duncan Ballash, Mark Bartlett, Jack Busby, Reid Condit, Russ Drinker, Rick Feldman, Karen Fiene, Bruce Fukuji, John Haag, Noreen Hughes, John McCaffrey, Jim McLane, Lisa Padilla, Cathy Schwabe, Thomas Simmons, William Tobiasson, Susan Vutz, Pierre Zetterberg

CIVIL, MARINE, AND STRUCTURAL ENGINEER Rutherford & Chekene

ELECTRICAL ENGINEER Cammisa and Wipf

EXHIBIT DESIGN Monterey Bay Aquarium Exhibit Group

LIFE-SUPPORT Enartec

MECHANICAL AND PLUMBING ENGINEER Guttmann & MacRitchie

PROJECT Rhodes/Dahl

CLIENT Monterey Bay Aquarium Foundation

PHOTOGRAPHY Peter Aaron/ESTO

UNIVERSITY OF CALIFORNIA LIBRARY & CENTER FOR KNOWLEDGE MANAGEMENT UC SAN FRANCISCO

ARCHITECT Esherick Homsey Dodge & Davis, San Francisco, CA

PRINCIPAL-IN-CHARGE Chuck Davis

PROJECT MANAGER Ed Rubin

PROJECT ARCHITECT Dave Deppen

PROJECT TEAM Mark Bartlett, Rick Feldman, Karen Fiene, Yuko Fukami, Charles Held, Richard Hocking, Noreen Hughes, Rapheal Olguin, Pierre Zetterberg

ELECTRICAL ENGINEER Cammisa and Wipf

INTERIORS Simon Martin-Vegue Winklestein Moris

LANDSCAPE Nishita and Carter

LIBRARY Gloria Novak

LIGHTING Architectural Lighting Design

STRUCTURAL AND CIVIL ENGINEER Rutherford & Chekene

MECHANICAL ENGINEER Guttmann & MacRichie

CLIENT University of California, San Francisco

PHOTOGRAPHY Peter Aaron/ESTO

UNIVERSITY OF CALIFORNIA SCIENCE LIBRARY UC SANTA CRUZ

ARCHITECT Esherick Homsey Dodge & Davis, San Francisco, CA

PRINCIPAL-IN-CHARGE Chuck Davis
PROJECT MANAGER Todd Sklar
PROJECT TEAM Mark Bartlett, Reid Condit, Ken Hammons,
Jay Raskin, Margret Tighe, David Vogel, Pierre Zetterberg
CIVIL ENGINEER Bestor Engineers, Inc.
ELECTRICAL ENGINEER Cammisa and Wipf
LANDSCAPE ARCHITECTURE Nishita and Carter
STRUCTURAL ENGINEER Rutherford & Chekene
MECHANICAL ENGINEER Guttmann & MacRichie
CLIENT University of California, Santa Cruz
PHOTOGRAPHY Peter Aaron/ESTO: p. 39, 40, 42, 43;
Doug Salin: p. 41

UNIVERSITY OF CALIFORNIA
MAIN LIBRARY COMPLEX
UC BERKELEY
ARCHITECT Esherick Homsey Dodge & Davis, San Francisco, CA
PRINCIPAL-IN-CHARGE Chuck Davis
PROJECT MANAGER Ed Dean
PROJECT ARCHITECT Paul Halajian
PROJECT TEAM Duncan Ballash, Mark Bartlett, Troy Bassett, David
Fawcett, Rick Feldman, Bruce Fukuji, Charles Held, Ashoke Kerr,
Jack Lamb, John McCafferey, Craig Murayama, Paul Roberts,
Virginia Rocha, Thomas Simmons, Mitchell Tobias, David Vogel,
Pierre Zetterberg
CIVIL ENGINEER Kennedy-Jenks-Chilton, Inc.
LANDSCAPE ARCHITECTURE Nishita and Carter
LIGHTING Luminar
STRUCTURAL ENGINEER Rutherford & Chekene
MEP ENGINEER Gayner Engineers
CLIENT University of California, Berkeley
PHOTOGRAPHY Peter Aaron/ESTO: p. 49 (top), 50 (bottom), 51;
Mark Citret: p. 45, 46, 47, 49 (bottom), 50 (top)

JOHN G. SHEDD AQUARIUM
FACILITY MASTER PLAN
CHICAGO, ILLINOIS
ARCHITECT Esherick Homsey Dodge & Davis, Chicago, IL
PRINCIPAL-IN-CHARGE Chuck Davis
PROJECT DIRECTOR Marc L'Italien
ASSOCIATE ARCHITECT Perkins & Will, Chicago, IL
PRINCIPAL-IN-CHARGE Ralph Johnson
LIFE-SUPPORT SYSTEMS Enartec
LIGHTING Schuler & Shook, Inc.
STRUCTURAL ENGINEER Klein and Hoffman, Inc.
MEP ENGINEER Environmental Systems Design, Inc.
PROGRAM MANAGER McClier
CLIENT John G. Shedd Aquarium

JOHN G. SHEDD AQUARIUM
GO OVERBOARD!
CHICAGO, ILLINOIS
ARCHITECT Esherick Homsey Dodge & Davis, Chicago, IL
PRINCIPAL-IN-CHARGE Chuck Davis
PROJECT DESIGNER/PROJECT MANAGER Marc L'Italien
PROJECT ARCHITECT Pierre Zetterberg
PROJECT TEAM Glennis Briggs, Kim Swanson
ASSOCIATED ARCHITECT (RETAIL) Schwartz Architects, New York, NY
PRINCIPAL-IN-CHARGE Frederic Schwartz
ASSOCIATE-IN-CHARGE Paul Cali
SENIOR PROJECT DESIGNER Leslie Y. Ghym
PROJECT TEAM Bruno Arnold, Shane Braddock, Steven Petrides
LIGHTING Schuler & Shook, Inc.
STRUCTURAL ENGINEER Klein and Hoffman, Inc.
MEP ENGINEER Environmental Systems Design, Inc.
PROJECT MANAGER/CONTRACTOR MANAGEMENT McClier
CLIENT John G. Shedd Aquarium
PHOTOGRAPHY Doug Snower Photography

JOHN G. SHEDD AQUARIUM CARIBBEAN REEF EXHIBIT CHICAGO, ILLINOIS

ARCHITECT Esherick Homsey Dodge & Davis, Chicago, IL

PRINCIPAL-IN-CHARGE Chuck Davis

PROJECT DESIGNER/MANAGER Marc L'Italien

PROJECT ARCHITECT Pierre Zetterberg

PROJECT TEAM Robert Aydlett, Tannys Langdon, Kim Swanson

ASSOCIATE ARCHITECT Perkins & Will, Chicago, IL

PRINCIPAL-IN-CHARGE Ralph Johnson

PROJECT TEAM Curt Behnke

ELECTRICAL ENGINEER Spectrum Engineering

GENERAL CONTRACTOR Turner Construction

GRAPHIC DESIGN Shedd Aquarium Planning and Design Department

LIFE-SUPPORT SYSTEMS Enartec

LIGHTING Schuler & Shook, Inc.

STRUCTURAL ENGINEER Klein and Hoffman, Inc.

MEP ENGINEER Environmental Systems Design, Inc.

PROGRAM MANAGER McClier

CLIENT John G. Shedd Aquarium

PHOTOGRAPHY Peter Aaron/ESTO

JOHN G. SHEDD AQUARIUM AMAZON RISING EXHIBIT CHICAGO, ILLINOIS

ARCHITECT Esherick Homsey Dodge & Davis, Chicago, IL

PRINCIPAL-IN-CHARGE Chuck Davis

PROJECT DIRECTOR Marc L'Italien

PROJECT MANAGER Anne Wattenberg

PROJECT DESIGNER Tannys Langdon

PROJECT ARCHITECT Susan Hagerty

PROJECT TEAM Chris Hoyt, Pierre Zetterberg

ASSOCIATE ARCHITECT Perkins & Will, Chicago, IL

PRINCIPAL-IN-CHARGE Ralph Johnson

PROJECT TEAM Cengiz Yetken

EXHIBIT PRODUCTION AND COORDINATION Esherick Homsey Dodge & Davis, Chicago, IL

PROJECT MANAGER Marjorie Brownstein

PROJECT ARCHITECT Tomislav Pejic

EXHIBIT DESIGN, GRAPHIC DESIGN Shedd Aquarium Planning and Design Department

GENERAL CONTRACTOR Turner Construction

LIFE-SUPPORT SYSTEMS Enartec

LIGHTING Schuler & Shook, Inc.

STRUCTURAL ENGINEER Klein and Hoffman, Inc.; Rutherford & Chekene

MEP ENGINEER Environmental Systems Design, Inc.

PROGRAM MANAGER McClier

CLIENT John G. Shedd Aquarium

PHOTOGRAPHY Steve Hall/Hedrich Blessing: p. 65, 66; Doug Snower Photography: p. 67

AQUARIUM OF THE PACIFIC LONG BEACH, CALIFORNIA

ARCHITECT Esherick Homsey Dodge & Davis, San Francisco, CA

DESIGN PRINCIPAL Chuck Davis

PROJECT MANAGER Scott Dennis

PROJECT TEAM Alexander Chun, Steve Dangermond, Toby Engelberg, Rick Feldman, Orla Huq, David Maglaty, Kim Swanson

ASSOCIATE ARCHITECT HOK

CIVIL ENGINEER Moffit and Nichol Engineers

CONTRACTOR Turner Construction

DEVELOPER Kajima International, Inc.

EXHIBIT DESIGNER Joseph A. Wetzel Associates

GENERAL CONTRACTOR Turner Construction

LANDSCAPE Fong and Associates

LIFE-SUPPORT SYSTEMS PC Aquatics

LIGHTING Gallegos Lighting Design

STRUCTURAL ENGINEER Rutherford & Chekene

MEP ENGINEER Syska and Hennessy
CLIENT City of Long Beach
PHOTOGRAPHY Timothy Hursley

PUBLICIS & HAL RINEY HEADQUARTERS SAN FRANCISCO, CALIFORNIA

ARCHITECT Esherick Homsey Dodge & Davis, San Francisco, CA
DESIGN PRINCIPAL Chuck Davis
PROJECT ARCHITECT/DESIGNER Briggs MacDonald
PROJECT TEAM Tom Heffernan, Michelle Hill, Alexandra McClellan, Hope Mitnick, Amy Storek, Jiaqi Wu
GRAPHICS Michael Cummings, Marianne Kelley, Suzan Zuckert
ELECTRICAL ENGINEER Decker Electric Co., Inc.; Randall Lamb Associates
LIGHTING Architectural Lighting Design
STRUCTURAL ENGINEER GFDS Engineers
MECHANICAL ENGINEER ACCO
CLIENT Publicis & Hal Riney
PHOTOGRAPHY Richard Barnes

TENDERLOIN SCHOOL AND COMMUNITY CENTER SAN FRANCISCO, CALIFORNIA

ARCHITECT Esherick Homsey Dodge & Davis, San Francisco, CA
PRINCIPAL-IN-CHARGE Joseph Esherick
PROJECT MANAGER Jennifer Devlin
PROJECT TEAM Toby Engelberg, Sabra Hattner, Soo Zee Park, David Rizzoli, Scott Shell, Kim Swanson, Pierre Zetterberg
ASSOCIATE ARCHITECT Barcelon & Jang
ELECTRICAL ENGINEER Pete O. Lapid and Associates
LANDSCAPE ARCHITECTURE Patricia O'Brien

MECHANICAL ENGINEER Tommy Siu and Associates
STRUCTURAL ENGINEER Structural Design Engineers
CLIENT San Francisco Unified School District
PHOTOGRAPHY Peter Aaron/ESTO: p. 83, 84 (bottom right), 88; Mark Darley/ESTO: p. 89; Ethan Kaplan: p. 84 (top, bottom left), 85

EXPLORIS RALEIGH, NORTH CAROLINA

ARCHITECT Clearscapes, PA, Raleigh, NC
PRINCIPAL-IN-CHARGE Steven D. Schuster
DESIGN PRINCIPAL Thomas H. Sayre
PROJECT ARCHITECTS Sarah H. Drake, Elias J. Torre
PROJECT TEAM Joseph D. Fenton
ASSOCIATE ARCHITECT Esherick Homsey Dodge & Davis, San Francisco, CA/Chicago, IL
SENIOR DESIGN PRINCIPAL Edward Rubin
PROJECT DESIGNER/PROJECT MANAGER Marc L'Italien
PROJECT ARCHITECT Pierre Zetterberg
PROJECT TEAM Paul Halajian, Calvin Hao, Thomas Robinson, Amy Taylor, David Vogel
EXHIBIT DESIGN Krent/Paffett Associates, Inc.; Design & Communication, Inc.
GENERAL CONTRACTOR MLB Industries
LIGHTING Gallegos Lighting Design
STRUCTURAL ENGINEER Lysaght & Associates, Inc.
MEP ENGINEER DS Atlantic, Inc.
CLIENT Exploris/Wake County Construction Management
PHOTOGRAPHY Doug Snower Photography

EXPLORIS
EXPLORISTORE
RALEIGH, NORTH CAROLINA

ARCHITECT Clearscapes, PA, Raleigh, NC

PRINCIPAL-IN-CHARGE Steven D. Schuster

DESIGN PRINCIPAL Thomas H. Sayre

PROJECT ARCHITECT Elias J. Torre

PROJECT TEAM Joseph D. Fenton

ASSOCIATE ARCHITECT Esherick Homsey Dodge & Davis, Chicago, IL

PRINCIPAL-IN-CHARGE Edward Rubin

PROJECT DESIGNER/PROJECT MANAGER Marc L'Italien

PROJECT ARCHITECT Mark Ashby

PROJECT TEAM Sarah Lavery

GENERAL CONTRACTOR J.C. Edwards General Contractors

LIGHTING Schuler & Shook, Inc.

STRUCTURAL ENGINEER Lysaght & Associates, Inc.

MEP ENGINEER DS Atlantic, Inc.

CLIENT Exploris/Wake County Construction Management

CLIENT TEAM Alan Daniels, Director of Exploris Enterprises

PHOTOGRAPHY Doug Snower Photography

BROOKFIELD ZOO
HABITAT AFRICA! — THE FOREST
BROOKFIELD, ILLINOIS

ARCHITECT Esherick Homsey Dodge & Davis, Chicago, IL

PRINCIPAL-IN-CHARGE Chuck Davis

PROJECT DESIGNER/MANAGER Marc L'Italien

PROJECT ARCHITECT Marjorie Brownstein

ZOO CONSULTANT Karen Fiene

DESIGN TEAM Mark Ashby, Sarah Lavery

EXHIBIT DESIGN Esherick Homsey Dodge & Davis, San Francisco, CA

PROJECT MANAGER Noreen Hughes

PROJECT TEAM Hope Mitnick, Henry Rollman

GENERAL CONTRACTOR GC International

LANDSCAPE AND EXTERIOR EXHIBITS MESA

STRUCTURAL ENGINEER Klein and Hoffman, Inc.

MEP ENGINEER Environmental Systems Design, Inc.

PROJECT MANAGER/CONTRACT MANAGEMENT McClier

CLIENT The Chicago Zoological Society

PHOTOGRAPHY Doug Snower Photography

1001 EMERSON
PALO ALTO, CALIFORNIA

ARCHITECT Esherick Homsey Dodge & Davis, San Francisco, CA

PROJECT ARCHITECT/DESIGNER Cathy Schwabe

PROJECT TEAM Shannon Ashmore, Robert Aydlett, Tom Blessing, Yung Chang, Sharon Nakatani, Mireille Roddier, Kate Simonen

GENERAL CONTRACTOR Drew Maran Construction/Design

ENERGY Gabel Dodd and Davis Energy Group

INTERIORS Futon Cheng/Sandra Slater

KITCHEN DESIGN AND WATER SCULPTURE Cheng Design

LANDSCAPE Cheryl Barton

LIGHTING Axiom Design

STRUCTURAL ENGINEER GFDS

PHOTOVOLTAIC DESIGN Light Energy Systems

CLIENT Sandra Slater

PHOTOGRAPHY David Wakely

NATIONAL MUSEUM OF MARINE
BIOLOGY/AQUARIUM
KENTING NATIONAL PARK
TAIWAN R.O.C.

ARCHITECT Esherick Homsey Dodge & Davis, San Francisco, CA

SENIOR DESIGN PRINCIPAL Chuck Davis

PRINCIPAL-IN-CHARGE Edward Rubin

PROJECT MANAGER/PROJECT DESIGNER Marc L'Italien
PROJECT ARCHITECT/PHASE 1 Russ Drinker
PROJECT ARCHITECT/PHASE 2 David Vogel
JOB CAPTAIN/PHASE 1 Pierre Zetterberg
PROJECT TEAM Nathalie Colodny, André Debar, Tony Duncan,
Brian Feagans, Julia Hawkinson, Szufu Jiang, John McCaffrey,
Tom Monahan, Stacie Velten Remy, Thomas Robinson,
Tom Simmons, Michael Tauber, Mitchell Tobias
ARCHITECT OF RECORD Haigo Shen & Associates, Taipei; J.J. Pan
and Partners, Taipei
ARCHITECTURAL AND EXHIBIT LIGHTING Gallegos Lighting Design
ELECTRICAL ENGINEER EISI; Leader Engineering Consultants
EXHIBIT DESIGN Joseph A. Wetzel Associates, Inc.
LANDSCAPE ARCHITECT Wallace Roberts & Todd
LIFE-SUPPORT SYSTEMS Montgomery Watson
MASTER PLAN COORDINATION Leo A. Daly, Omaha, NE
STRUCTURAL, MECHANICAL, PLUMBING, AND CIVIL ENGINEER KCMI
MEP ENGINEER I.S. Lin and Associates
PROJECT MANAGEMENT KCMI, Seattle; KCMI, Kaohsiung
STRUCTURAL T.Y. Lin Taiwan
CLIENT National Museum of Marine Biology/Aquarium Preparatory
Office
PHOTOGRAPHY Peter Aaron/ESTO

ACKNOWLEDGEMENTS

It was an honor to organize this volume, although it was somewhat of a daunting task considering that no book has ever been published exclusively on the work of Joseph Esherick or EHDD. In light of the landmark projects that have comprised the firm's prolific output and contributed so profoundly to the Bay Area's architectural history, this is unfortunate. I am grateful to have had this opportunity and hope others follow my lead. This volume was not intended as a comprehensive monograph, but as a sampling of selected projects completed between 1984 and 2000, placed in the context of EHDD's rich history.

EHDD has been a collaborative enterprise from the time Joe Esherick opened the practice in 1946. As such, I wish to thank all of our clients—individuals and institutions—who have challenged us to design thoughtful projects through the years. We have always been grateful to our many consultants and contractors who have helped shape the work, and whose contributions often strengthened our original design intent.

I would like to recognize EHDD's dedicated staff, both past and present. Without their hard work, long hours, and commitment to design excellence—despite the effects on their personal lives—the work included in this volume would never have been possible.

I wish to thank Chuck Davis for his vision, his constant support, his editorial assistance, and his reminiscences about the work. Chuck took time away from his own projects and family to provide his vision of what this book should be.

I thank the principals at EHDD for their financial and emotional support; special thanks go to George Homsey and Peter Dodge for their recollections of projects, clients, and events which occurred long before databases. I extend my gratitude to Peter Dodge for his care in researching archival drawings, photographs, and correspondence to set the record straight where discrepancies existed. I am indebted to Louis Roach, Associate Professor of Architecture at the University of Illinois at Chicago and early employee of Joseph Esherick, for his critical review of my essays.

Thanks to Raul Barreneche for contributing his wonderful essay on EHDD. Although many have come before him—writing articles primarily about Joseph Esherick or critiquing specific proj-ects, project types, or periods of the firm's history—Raul is the first to write an essay about the current practice while underscoring the firm's continuing connections with its past.

I am also indebted to Suzanne Riess for her 1996 publication, *Joseph Esherick: an Oral History*, a document that proved invaluable to my research on the early work of the firm. I am equally indebted to those at EHDD who contributed their time and writing skills to the development of project statements. These individuals met deadlines and gathered the necessary data and documents for their respective projects.

Many thanks go to the distinguished photographers who have contributed so much to our projects through their images: Peter Aaron, Wayne Andrews, Richard Barnes, Mark Citret, Mark Darley, Steve Hall, Timothy Hursley, Ethan Kaplan, Rob Levine, Kathleen Olson, Doug Salin, Doug Snower, David Wakely, and various EHDD architects, including Peter Dodge, George Homsey, and Debra Stinski.

My thanks go to Robert Aydlet and Susan Millhouse in the San Francisco office for their insights on the work and oversight of all the coordination efforts out west, and to Kari Holmquist for her copyediting work. I also want to acknowledge Judith Paquette's extensive research assistance, enthusiasm, and dedication to this project. Thanks to Saskia van Dijl for her positive attitude and persistence in promoting the work of EHDD to the general public. She has nurtured the talents of the firm's younger designers through the years.

I wish to thank my entire staff at the Chicago office for their patience while I diverted much of my attention away from ongoing projects and concentrated on this publication. I thank Katrina Swanson for her help with the correspondence. I am indebted to Chris Hoyt for his help in coordinating documents and photography, and his assistance in overseeing the production of new drawings needed to tell the story of the firm. I also wish to thank Marjorie Brownstein for her thoughtful edits to my drafts.

Thanks to Frederic Schwartz for his long-lasting friendship, his memories of one Professor Esherick, and his advice on publish-ing books.

At Edizioni Press, I wish to thank Sarah Palmer. I am also grateful to Jamie Schwartz for her constant guidance throughout this process and her editorial skills. I wish to thank the editorial director, Anthony Iannacci, for his ever-thoughtful suggestions on content, format, and images, and for his commitment to this volume.

Finally a warm and heartfelt thanks to Alan Buchsbaum and Joseph Esherick. These two mentors taught me that it is possible to design critically acclaimed buildings and places while allowing the imperfections and lighter side of life to color the work. They remained consummate individuals in a profession often swayed by fashion and trend.

MARC L'ITALIEN